gsw hauptverwaltung
berlin
sauerbruch hutton
architekten

gsw headquarters
berlin
sauerbruch hutton
architects

AXEL SPRINGER VERLA

gsw hauptverwaltung berlin sauerbruch hutton architekten

gsw headquarters berlin sauerbruch hutton architects

Lars Müller Publishers

Friedrichstraße
Friedrichstraße
PIZZA

AXEL SPRINGER VERLAG
WELT

Die GSW Hauptverwaltung ist eine Assemblage aus fünf im Charakter eigenständigen Gebäuden. Diese Vielfalt von Elementen entstand im Eingehen auf die unterschiedlichen typologischen und morphologischen Bedingungen des Standorts, im Übergang zwischen der sogenannten nördlichen und der südlichen Friedrichstadt im Zentrum Berlins.
Insbesondere im Rahmen der Diskussion um die Rekonstruktion der einst geteilten Stadt artikuliert sich hier eine eigene Urbanität, die das auf Grund seiner wechselhaften Geschichte entstandene Konglomerat der Stadt Berlin als Grundstruktur akzeptiert.
Geschichte ist ein dynamischer Prozess, der sichtbare Spuren hinterlässt. Der Gedanke, mit diesen Spuren wie mit anderen vorgefundenen Randbedingungen konstruktiv und kreativ umzugehen, bildet die Grundlage dieses Entwurfes.
Mit einem bereits 1990 entwickelten Niedrigenergiekonzept weist der Bau in die Zukunft. Mit seiner eigenständigen Ästhetik fordert er zu Beginn des 21. Jahrhunderts die Rückkehr einer sinnlichen Architektur.

The GSW Headquarters Building is an assemblage of five distinct volumes. This variety of elements allows a response to the different typological and morphological conditions of the ensemble's location between the southern and northern parts of the so-called *Friedrichstadt* in the centre of Berlin. Within the discussion about the reconstruction of the once-divided capital, this project articulates a response to the city which accepts Berlin's historical conglomerate as a structural principle. History is seen as a dynamic process which leaves its traces. The intention to work with these traces – as with any other condition of the context – in a constructive and creative way is the underlying principle of this scheme. With its low-energy concept the building leads into the future, and with its idiosyncratic aesthetics it demands the return of a sensual architecture at the beginning of the 21st century.

Mo - Fr 7 - 18 h
Krankenfahrzeuge
TAXI frei
Be- und Entladen

Um die Geschichte des Grundstücks Kochstrasse 22/23 zu verstehen, muss man die Geschichte der Stadt Berlin kennen. Die Recherche zeigt eine relativ schnelle, extrem wechselhafte Abfolge unterschiedlicher Stadtideen seit ca. 1700. Die barocken Stadterweiterungen der nördlichen und der südlichen Friedrichstadt wurden im späten 19. und frühen 20. Jahrhundert zum *steinernen Berlin* verdichtet. Die Bombardements von 1945, der Wiederaufbau in Ost und West, der Einschnitt der Mauer und die Internationale Bauausstellung in den 80er-Jahren führten dann zu der Stadtgestalt, die wir zu Beginn des Projektes vorfanden.
Die Gleichzeitigkeit der Spuren vieler Entwicklungsstadien weist die Friedrichstadt in besonderem Masse als eine reichhaltige Landschaft aus, die die soziale, kulturelle und politische Geschichte der Stadt verkörpert.

City Landscape

To understand the history of the site on Kochstrasse one has to be aware of the history of the city of Berlin.
The research shows a relatively rapid, very varied sequence of different urban ideas to have taken shape since ca. 1700.
The baroque city extensions of the northern and the southern *Friedrichstadt* were to become the dense *stony Berlin* of the late 19th and early 20th centuries. The bombardments of 1945, the post-war reconstruction in East and West, the incision of the Wall and the 1980's International Building Exhibition finally lead to the heterogeneous urban structure which was to be found at the start of the project.
The simultaneous traces of the various stages of development show *Friedrichstadt* as a rich urban landscape which embodies the social, cultural and political history of this city.

B·Z
die größte
Zeitung
Berlins!

BUS

Ullsteinhaus an der Ecke Kochstrasse/Charlottenstrasse im Jahre 1910
Ullsteinhaus on the corner of Kochstrasse and Charlottenstrasse in 1910

Ullsteinhaus, 1946
Ullsteinhaus, 1946

Perspektive des GGZ (Graphisches und Gewerbezentrum), Architekten Schwebes/Schoszberger/Noth, 1956
Perspective of the GGZ (Graphisches und Gewerbezentrum), architects Schwebes/Schoszberger/Noth, 1956

GGZ von der Ecke Kochstrasse/Charlottenstrasse, 1961
GGZ from the corner of Kochstrasse and Charlottenstrasse, 1961

GGZ von der Charlottenstrasse, 1961
GGZ from Charlottenstrasse, 1961

Checkpoint Charlie, Grenzübergang nach Ost-Berlin, 1968
Checkpoint Charlie, border crossing to East-Berlin, 1968

Grundsteinlegung des GGZ, 1957
Foundation stone ceremony for the GGZ, 1957

Das GGZ als Sprachrohr zum Osten, 1962
The GGZ as *Newsreader* billboard towards the east, 1962

Die Mauer und ihre Grenzanlagen in der Friedrichstadt
The Berlin Wall and it's fortifications, in Friedrichstadt

GGZ von der Ecke Charlottenstrasse/Besselstrasse, 1963
GGZ from the corner of Charlottenstrasse and Besselstrasse, 1963

1

2

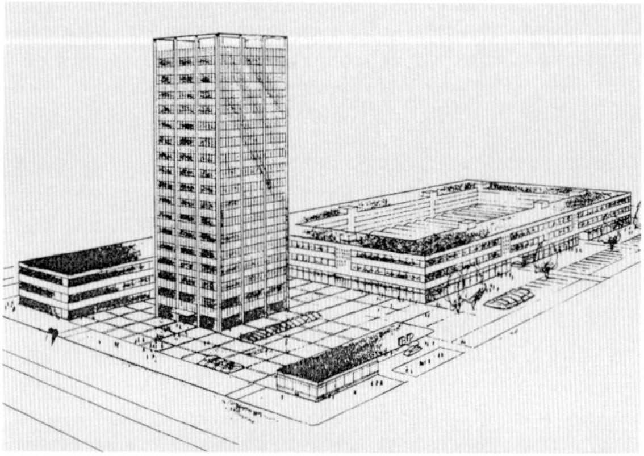
3

4

5

6

7

8

9

10

Plan von der Königl. Residentz Stadt Berlin, 1723, gezeichnet von G. Dusableau
Map of the *Königl. Residentz Stadt Berlin* (Royal Residential City), 1723, drawn by G. Dusableau

Die versteinerte Kabinettsordre Gemälde von Dismas Dägen, vermutlich vor 1735
***The petrified cabinet order* painting by Dismas Dägen, probably before 1735**

Ausschnitt aus *Plan de la Ville de Berlin* von Graf von Schmettau, 1748
Detail from *Plan de la Ville de Berlin* by Graf von Schmettau, 1748

Ausschnitt aus dem *Liebenow-Plan*, 1888
Detail from the *Liebenow plan*, 1888

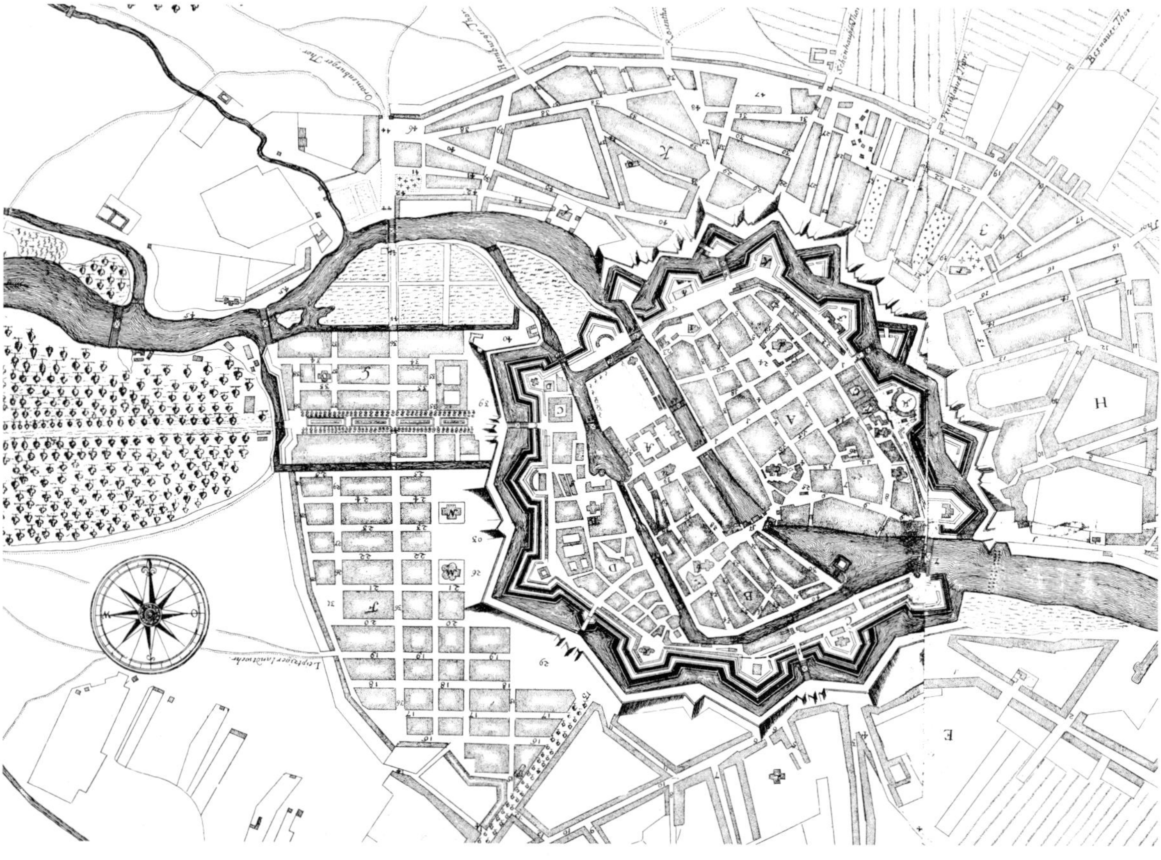

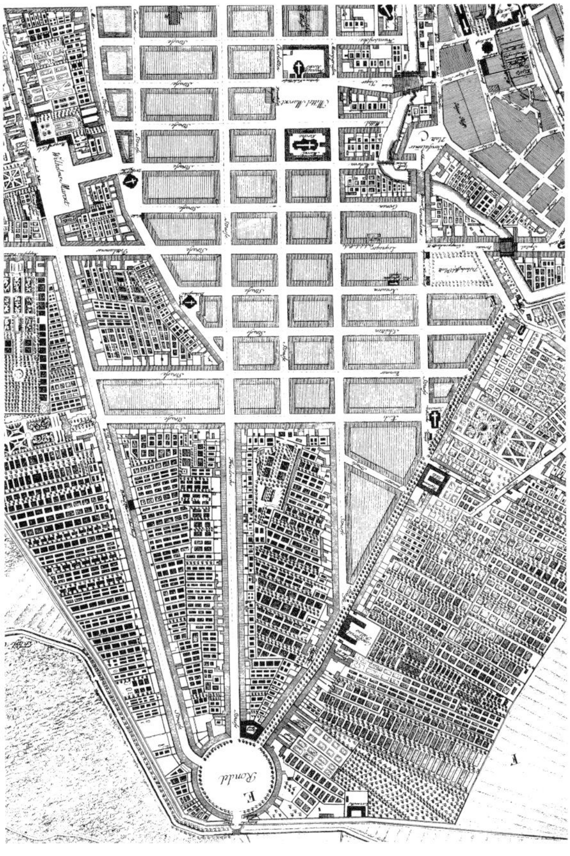

Hedwigs K.
Strasse
Französische K.
Gensdarmen
Königl. Schauspielhs.
Markt
Strasse
Neue K.
Ste.

Luftaufnahme des Grundstücks um 1925
Aerial view of the site, circa 1925

Luftaufnahme des Grundstücks, 1945
Aerial view of the site, 1945

Luftaufnahme GGZ mit Blick nach Osten um 1962
Aerial view of the GGZ looking towards East Berlin, circa 1962

Luftaufnahme Friedrichstadt, 1953
Aerial view of Friedrichstadt, 1953

Luftaufnahme Bezirk Mitte von Südwesten, 1971,
Hochhäuser an der Leipziger Strasse im Bau
Aerial view looking towards Berlin Mitte (East Berlin), 1971, with the high-rise buildings on Leipziger Strasse under construction

Luftaufnahme südliche Friedrichstadt von Süden um 1975
Aerial view of southern Friedrichstadt looking north, circa 1975

Südliche Friedrichstadt, Ausschnitt aus dem Stadtmodell
der internationalen Bauausstellung (IBA), 1984
Southern Friedrichstadt, a detail view from the city planning model of the International Building Exhibition (IBA), 1984

Blick nach Osten, 1991
View towards the east, 1991

Wettbewerb

Im Herbst 1990 hatte die GSW, Gemeinnützige Siedlungs- und Wohnungsbaugesellschaft, Berlin mbH, einen beschränkten Wettbewerb unter sechs Architekten für den Neubau und die Erweiterung ihrer Hauptverwaltung an der Kochstrasse ausgelobt. Die Ausschreibung verlangte eine Erweiterung des bestehenden Gebäudes um 19000 m^2 Büro- und Ladenflächen.
Der Wettbewerb hatte – als einer der ersten nach der Wende – ein grosses Gebäude in der Berliner Innenstadt zum Thema und beschäftigte sich implizit mit der Frage des Zusammenwachsens der beiden Stadthälften, hier der nördlichen und der südlichen Friedrichstadt.
Die Jury, bestehend aus dem Bauherrn, vier freien Architekten sowie Vertretern des Bezirks Kreuzberg und des Senats, entschied sich im Dezember 1990, eine zweite Bearbeitungsphase zwischen zwei Teilnehmern durchzuführen. Im März 1991 wurde dem Entwurf von sauerbruch hutton architekten einstimmig der erste Preis verliehen.

Competition

In autumn 1990 GSW, *Gemeinnützige Siedlungs- und Wohnungsbaugesellschaft, Berlin mbH* (Berlin's largest housing association), held a competition amongst six architects for the design of an extension to their headquarters building on Kochstrasse. The brief asked for 19,000 sqm of offices and shops.
This competition was one of the first for a major building in the historic centre of Berlin since the reunification, and implicitly addressed the question of the re-joining of the two city-halves – in this case the northern and southern parts of *Friedrichstadt*.
The jury, consisting of the client, four independant architects as well as representatives of the Borough of Kreuzberg and the Berlin Senate, decided in December 1990 to hold a second round between two of the competitors. In March 1991 the design by sauerbruch hutton architects was unanimously awarded first prize.

Erläuterungsbericht Februar 1991
Auszug

Funktionale Organisation des Gebäudes

Horizontale Erweiterbarkeit

Durch die direkte Anbindung der neuen Scheibe an den bestehenden Turm bietet sich für jedes Hochhausgeschoss eine horizontale Erweiterbarkeit um ca. 100 %. Vertikal kann die neue Scheibe an jeder beliebigen Stelle abgetrennt werden, so dass z. B. nur die oberen zehn Geschosse von der GSW genutzt werden, während die unteren acht vermietet sind.

Grundrissflexibilität

Innerhalb der Scheibe sind die Geschossgrundrisse frei einteilbar. Trennwände können im 1-m-Raster an jeder beliebigen Stelle zwischen der Westfassade und der internen *Arkade* des konstruktiven *Rückgrats* gestellt werden, um Bürozellen beliebiger Grösse abzutrennen. Ebenso kann der Raum ununterbrochen als Grossraumbüro genutzt werden.

Erdgeschossnutzungen

Das Erdgeschoss bietet im Bereich des Flachbaus an der Kochstrasse eine Anzahl von vermietbaren Ladenflächen; im Bereich des dreigeschossigen *Pavillonbaus* auf der Westseite sollten die leicht zugänglichen Erdgeschossflächen evtl. als Mieterberatungsstelle der GSW genutzt werden. Zwischen Alt- und Neubau ist wie im Wettbewerbsentwurf eine Eingangshalle vorgesehen. Der ursprünglich pavillonartig angelegte Konferenzraum ist auf Wunsch des Auslobers durch eine multifunktionale *Halle* ersetzt worden, die durch Abteilung sowohl als Ausstellungsfläche als auch als Konferenzraum o.ä. zu nutzen ist.

Flachbauten

Die Flachbauten an Koch- und Charlottenstrasse bieten in den beiden Obergeschossen ebenfalls frei einteilbare Büroflächen, die zur Vermietung zur Verfügung stehen.

Die wohltemperierte Arbeitswelt – Überlegungen zur Umgebungsqualität in und um das neue Gebäude

Umweltbewusstsein

In einer Zeit, in der sich die Gesellschaft stärker denn je der Bedingungen der Umwelt bewusst ist und der rationelle Umgang mit Energie und natürlichen Ressourcen zur Überlebensfrage geworden ist, kann sich gerade die Architektur dieser Problematik nicht entziehen und ist zum Eingehen auf natürliche Umweltbedingungen und zum intelligenten Umgang mit neuer und erprobter Technologie herausgefordert. Unsere Überlegungen galten der

Competition Report Febuary 1991
Extract

Functional Organisation of the Building

Horizontal Extendability
Due to the direct connection of the new slab to the old tower, each existing floor can be extended by 100%. Vertically the slab can be divided at any point so that, for example, only the ten upper floors could be used by GSW, whilst the remaining eight below could be let.

Flexibility of Plan
Within the slab the floor plans can be divided as required. Dividing walls to create office rooms of various sizes can be placed at any point on a 1 m grid between the west façade and the internal *arcade* of the structural backbone. Equally the space can be used undivided as an open-plan office.

Ground Floor
The ground floor of the low building along Kochstrasse offers a number of shop units; whilst the ground floor of the easily accessible *pavilion* on the west side could be used as GSW's tenant advice centre. Between the old and the new buildings, as in the (first phase of the) competition design, lies the entrance hall. The conference room (which was originally planned as a type of pavilion) has – following the client's request – been replaced by a multi-functional hall which can be used for various activities.

Low Buildings
The low buildings along Kochstrasse and Charlottenstrasse both offer freely divisible office space on the two upper floors which is available to let.

The Well-tempered Office – Proposals for Environmental Quality in and around the New Building

Environmental Consciousness
At a time when society is more than ever aware of the condition of the environment, and when a sensible approach to energy and natural resources has become a question of survival, architecture cannot evade these problems and is challenged to address environmental issues with intelligent use of both, new and tested technologies. Our considerations were concerned with:

- the maximum use of passive energy through orientation (to the extent permitted by the urban context),

– maximalen passiven Energienutzung durch Orientierung (soweit im städtischen Kontext möglich),
– der Kontrolle der um das bestehende Hochhaus existierenden Windsituation,
– der maximalen Ausnutzung des Tageslichts,
– dem maximalen Luftaustausch in Arbeitsräumen ohne Beeinträchtigung durch Zug und Kaltluft,
– der maximalen individuellen Kontrolle der Umweltbedingungen am Arbeitsplatz.

Orientierung
Durch richtige Orientierung der Hochhausscheibe wird die optimale passive Nutzung von Solarenergie erreicht: Während die schmalen Seiten des Gebäudes nach Norden und Süden gerichtet sind nutzt vor allem die westliche *Breitseite* die niedere Westsonne. Die Aussenräume östlich und westlich des Gebäudes sind jeweils von Morgen- bzw. Nachmittagssonne beschienen.

Wind
Bei starkem Wind entstehen an den Kanten von Hochhäusern durch Druckunterschied Turbulenzen und Verstärkungen der Windkraft. Dies hat den positiven Effekt der Vermischung von Luftschichten, was vor allem an Smogtagen zur lokalen Verbesserung der Luftqualität führt. Als negatives Resultat treten verstärkte Windkräfte im Fussgängerbereich auf. Durch die Addition der Scheibe zum existierenden Turm entsteht ein geschützter Bereich im Osten des Gebäudes (Hauptwindrichtung: West). Der Fussgängerbereich im Westen wird durch Auskragungen im Bereich der Flachbauten geschützt, die zusammen eine Wind-*Rinne* bilden, die abfallende Winde auffängt und umleitet. Um den Effekt dieser Rinne im südlichen Bereich fortzusetzen und den Bereich zwischen GSW und GGZ zu schützen, ist im 3. OG der Scheibe zusätzlich ein Wind-*Spoiler* angebracht, der Winde über das Dach des GGZ umleitet. Ebenso trägt die Bepflanzung der beiden Aussenbereiche und der Blockpassage dazu bei, Fussgängerbereiche vor heftigem Wind zu schützen.

Energiesparen
Wir haben unseren Entwurf unter anderem mit dem Ziel überarbeitet, maximale Raumbehaglichkeit und Nutzungskomfort bei geringstmöglichem Energieverbrauch zu erreichen. Da jedoch die Verwirklichung intelligenter Energieeinsparungsmassnahmen auch von der Bereitschaft des Bauherrn abhängt, langfristige Investitionen zu tätigen, stellen wir drei Alternativen zur Wahl, die aufeinander aufbauen. Jede Alternative ist in sich vollständig und allein durchführbar; mit jedem Schritt wird jedoch die Energieeffizienz des Gebäudes gesteigert und damit die Belastung der Umwelt verringert.

Alternative I
Natürliche Querlüftung
Zunächst wird vorgeschlagen, den gesamten Baukörper mit einer Glashaut zu umgeben, um maximale Tageslichtnutzung und Energieeinsparung durch passive Nutzung von Solarenergie zu erreichen. Teile dieser Haut sind in transparenter Doppel- bzw. Dreifachverglasung, Teile in transluzenter Wärmedämmung vorgesehen. Die Westseite des Gebäudes ist durch eine Schicht von Schiebeläden vor extremer Sonneneinstrahlung geschützt. Die Lüftung der Räume geschieht durch das Öffnen der Fenster. Raumheizung und Warmwasserversorgung werden durch traditionelle Zentralheizung bzw. Fernheizung abgedeckt.

Alternative II
Natürliche Querlüftung mit Wärmerückgewinnung durch *Solarkamin*
Durch die Einführung einer zweiten Glashaut vor der Westfassade wird hier die Solarenergie in einem *Solarkamin* eingefangen und durch Rückgewinnung nutzbar gemacht: Durch natürlichen Auftrieb steigt die warme Luft in dieser Glasschicht bis zum Dach auf, wo die Wärme über Wärmetauscher oder

– the control of the current wind situation around the existing high-rise,
– the maximum use of daylight,
– the maximum rate of air exchange possible without the side-effects of drafts and cold air,
– the maximum control of environmental comfort for the individual at his/her workplace.

Orientation

Through the correct orientation of the high-rise slab optimal passive use of solar energy is achieved. While the narrow ends of the building are oriented north and south, the long west-facing façade can exploit the low angle of the western sun. The exterior spaces to the east and west of the building are oriented to the morning and afternoon sun respectively.

Wind

On windy days turbulence and an increase in windforce occur at the edges of skyscrapers. This has the positive effect of mixing layers of air, which particularly on days of high pollution leads to a local improvement in air quality. On the other hand increased winds affect the pedestrian level. The addition of the slab to the existing tower produces a sheltered area to the east of the building (main wind direction: west). The pedestrian area to the west is protected by cantilevers around the low buildings, together forming a *wind gutter* which collects and diverts downward wind. In order to continue the effect of this gutter to the south, and so to protect the area between GSW and GGZ, there is a *wind spoiler* on the third floor which diverts the wind over the roof of the GGZ. Equally the planting of both the exterior spaces and the *block passage* helps to protect these pedestrian areas from strong wind.

Energy Saving

One of the aims of our design was to achieve a maximum of interior comfort with the minimum possible expenditure of energy. As, however, the realisation of intelligent energy-saving measures is dependant upon the readiness of the client to make a long term investment, we are proposing three alternative solutions. Each of these is complete in itself and can be executed independently, or the alternatives can be used in combination. With each additional measure the energy-efficiency of the building is increased and so the load on the environment is correspondingly reduced.

Alternative I

Natural Ventilation

First of all it is proposed to enclose the complete volume of the new building with a glass skin, in order to maximise both energy savings through the passive use of solar energy and the use of daylight. Some parts of this skin are of transparent double or triple glazing, and other parts are of translucent insulation material. The west side of the building is protected from extremes of solar radiation by a layer of sliding shutters. The ventilation of the offices is achieved by opening windows. Heating and warm water are provided through traditional central and district heating respectively.

Alternative II

Natural Ventilation with energy reclaimed via a Thermal Flue

Through the placement of a second glass skin in front of the west façade the solar energy is caught in a thermal flue and can be made useful through the recovery of it's energy. With natural convection warm air rises in this glass layer up to the roof, where the heat is extracted, and by means of a heat exchanger or heat pump can contribute to the warm water or the heating of the building respectively. (The deployment of a heat pump can, without extra cost, be used to convert recovered heat into coolness for the summer.)

Wärmepumpen zur Unterstützung der Warmwasserversorgung sowie der Heizung des Hauses zugeführt werden kann. (Der Einsatz einer Wärmepumpe würde ohne Mehraufwand auch die Umwandlung der rückgewonnenen Wärme in Kühle für den Sommer ermöglichen.) Gleichzeitig zieht die aufsteigende Luft Abluft aus den Büroräumen und funktioniert als natürliche Belüftungsanlage. Die Intensität dieser Lüftung kann durch die Öffnung von Fenstern in den *Solarkamin* reguliert werden. Die Glashaut dient dann auch als Schutz, der die negativen Effekte von Fensterlüftung, nämlich das Eindringen von Wind und Kaltluft eliminiert. Die von uns vorgesehenen Sonnenschutzläden aus Lochblech sind ebenfalls im Glaspuffer untergebracht. Durch die Absorption von Wärme in diesen Blech-*Vorhängen* wird der Kamineffekt erhöht. Ausserdem sind die Läden damit vor Wind und Wetter geschützt.
Die Luftzufuhr geschieht auf der Ostseite über Öffnungen in der Fassade, wobei der Korridor als Verteiler und Wärmepuffer fungiert. Da diese Seite während der Büroarbeitszeiten praktisch immer vom Altbau verschattet ist, sind zusätzliche Sonnenschutzmassnahmen nicht notwendig.

Alternative III
Natürliche Entlüftung bei mechanischer Belüftung und Ausnutzung der Speichermasse der Primärkonstruktion.
Als Weiterentwicklung dieser Ideen schlagen wir die Qualitätskontrolle der Frischluft vor: Anstatt Frischluft direkt über die Fassade in das Gebäude einzuführen, wird zumindest ein Teil der Luft zentral auf dem Dach angesaugt, gereinigt, mit rückgewonnener Energie vorgewärmt oder -gekühlt und dann in die Büros verteilt.
Um Wärme (und Kühle) optimal in der ohnehin vorhandenen Masse der Konstruktion zu speichern, wird diese Frischluft in Hohlräumen innerhalb der Betonfertigteildecken verteilt. Damit können die Räume mit Billigstrom über Nacht vorgeheizt oder -gekühlt werden, was wiederum den Grad der Behaglichkeit und den Heizungs-/Kühlungsaufwand tagsüber verringern würde.

Der Genius loci als Identität – Städtebauliche Grundideen

Charme der 50er-Jahre
Bei der Recherche für dieses Projekt fanden wir in der Landesbildstelle Fotografien von der Grundsteinlegung der GGZ im Jahre 1957. Ein Foto zeigt Rudolf Ullstein, ca.80-jährig, umgeben von Willy Brandt als jungem Bürgermeister und Eleanor Dulles, der Schwester des damaligen amerikanischen Aussenministers. Die Prominenz ist umgeben von Berliner Politikern, Handwerkern und Bürgern.
Im Hintergrund eine der noch wenigen stehenden Ruinen.
Ebenso wie die heroische Fotografie des eben vollendeten Zentrums (komplett mit Isetta und Opel Rekord) scheint diese Szene gleichzeitig amüsant und berührend; der Wunsch, die extrem schwierige Realität der Nachkriegszeit zu meistern, die Sehnsucht nach einem radikalen Bruch mit der Vergangenheit und einem völligen Neuanfang, der unstillbare Optimismus, kombiniert mit bewusstem *Weltstädtertum* und vor allem tiefem Ernst.
Dennoch – trotz aller Kritik an dieser Zeit, trotz geschmäcklerischer Architektur und überspannter Bebauungspläne –, dies sind die Menschen, die Berlin nach dem Krieg wieder auf die Beine gebracht haben, und sie verdienen unseren Respekt.

At the same time the natural convection draws exhaust air from the offices, and functions as a natural ventilation system. The intensity of this ventilation can be controlled by the degree to which the windows are opened into the thermal flue.
The additional glass skin also offers protection which eliminates the negative effects of natural ventilation – that is the penetration of wind and cold air. The perforated metal solar shutters are likewise housed in this glass buffer zone and are so protected from wind and rain.
The absorption of heat by the metal surfaces of these shutters increases the effect of convection.
The air intake takes place on the east side via openings in the façade, whereby the corridor functions as both an air distribution zone and as a thermal buffer. While during office hours this side is virtually always in the shade of the existing building additional solar protection is unnecessary.

Alternative III
Natural air exhaust in combination with mechanical fresh air intake and exploitation of the thermal mass of the primary construction.
As a development of these ideas we propose to control the quality of the incoming air. Instead of introducing fresh air directly into the building from the façade, at least some of the incoming air will be drawn in at roof level, then cleaned and warmed (or cooled) using recovered energy before it's distribution into the offices.
In order to maximize the potential of the available mass of the construction, this incoming air is distributed into cavities within the precast concrete floors where the warmth (or coolness) is stored. In this way the rooms can be pre-heated (or pre-cooled) over night using cheap rate electricity, which in turn increases the comfort of the spaces and reduces the need for daytime heating (or cooling).

Genius Loci as Identity – Basic Ideas on Urban Development

The Charm of the Fifties
Whilst undertaking the research for this project we discovered photographs of the foundation stone ceremony of the GGZ from 1957 in the city archives. One photograph shows a ca. 80 year old Rudolf Ullstein surrounded by Willy Brandt as a young mayor and Eleanor Dulles, the sister of the American Foreign Minister of the time. The VIPs are surrounded by Berlin's politicians, craftspeople and citizens. The background shows one of the few remaining ruins.
Similar to the historic photograph of the just completed centre (GGZ) (complete with Isetta and Opel Rekord), this scene appears both amusing and touching; the desire to master the extremely difficult situation of the post-war times, the longing for a radical break with the past and a completely new beginning, the unquenchable optimism combined with self-consciously *Cosmopolitan* behaviour and above all deep seriousness.
Nevertheless – in spite of all the criticism of this period, in spite of tasteless architecture and over-ambitious development plans – these are the people who got Berlin on it's feet after the war and they deserve our respect.

Retroaktive Integration

Das GGZ, als Dokument dieser Zeit, verdient ebenso ernst genommen zu werden wie ein Friedrichstädtisches Haus aus dem 18. oder 19. Jahrhundert. Trotz seiner eher mittelmässigen Qualität ist seine Architektur Bestandteil der Friedrichstadt, seine Geschichte Bestandteil der Berliner Nachkriegsgeschichte und klarer Ausdruck der Sehnsüchte dieser Generation. Das Gebäude repräsentiert eine Stadtideologie, die bewusst mit dem historischen Muster bricht. Da diese Vision der modernen Stadt auf Grund des Mauerbaus nicht annähernd vollendet wurde, blieben die wenigen ‹ Pionier › -Gebäude immer Einzelgänger in der fragmentarischen Stadtstruktur. Nachdem die Mauer nun verschwunden und die Koexistenz der Gegensätze zur Notwendigkeit geworden ist, scheint es uns als städtebauliches Ziel der Veränderung des Graphischen und Gewerbezentrums angebracht, diesen Gebäudekomplex einzubinden und retrospektiv zu verwurzeln, anstatt ihn als Fremdkörper zu betonen. Unser Entwurf unternimmt es, sowohl auf die bestehenden Gebäude in ihrer Höhe einzugehen und sie durch Rahmung aufzuwerten als auch den Einzelkörper im Strassenplan zu verankern.

Manhattan

Bis zu einem gewissen Grad lässt sich die Friedrichstadt mit Manhattan vergleichen: Zum einen bildet ihr Grundriss eine prägnante Figur im Berliner Häusermeer, zum anderen hatte sie zumindest vor dem Krieg eine ähnliche Dichte und ausgesprochenen Geschäftsstadtcharakter. Darüber hinaus hat sich im Lauf der Geschichte zumindest in Teilen der Friedrichstadt ein Stadtmodell gebildet, das ähnlich dem Gridiron-Plan New Yorks auf einem dialektischen Konflikt zwischen Stadtgrundriss und Architektur beruht. Die Architekturlandschaft hat sich vom Korsett des Strassenrasters gelöst. Auf diesem *dritten Weg* wie es Manfredo Tafuri nennt, nähert sich die Friedrichstadt einem Stadtmodell, wo *die Freiheit, die dem einzelnen architektonischen Fragment zugestanden wird, sich in einen Kontext einbindet, der in seiner Form nicht vom einzelnen Fragment bestimmt ist.*

Dialektische Stadt

Insbesondere seit Ostberlin wieder auf offiziellen Karten dargestellt wird und in unseren Köpfen wieder als Bestandteil der Innenstadt existiert, ist die Korrespondenz einzelner Bauten über das Strassenraster hinweg offensichtlich. Dieser überörtliche Dialog ist (von der Mauer hervorgerufen) zum integralen Bestandteil der Friedrichstadt geworden und insbesondere im Falle des GGZ zu berücksichtigen. Unser Vorschlag versucht zum einen die collagenhafte Überlagerung von architektonischen Elementen aus der Geschichte zu thematisieren und fortzusetzen, zum anderen sehen wir seine städtebauliche Figur als ein direktes Resultat der dialektischen Koexistenz der geometrischen und der landschaftlichen Ordnung in diesem Teil der Stadt.

Retroactive Integration

The GGZ, as a document of this time, deserves to be taken just as seriously as a building in Friedrichstadt from the 18th or 19th centuries. In spite of it's rather mediocre quality, it's architecture is an integral part of Friedrichstadt, it's history is an integral part of Berlin's post-war history and a clear statement of the yearnings of this generation. The building represents an urban ideology which deliberately breaks with the historical context. Because this vision of the Modern City could not (even in part) be completed due to the building of the Wall, the few *Pioneer* buildings remained isolated in the fragmented city structure. Now that the Wall has gone and the coexistence of opposites has become a necessity, it appeared to us to be appropriate to integrate the building complex of the GGZ into the city fabric and to lend it roots retrospectively, instead of stressing it's alien character. Our design reacts to the height of the existing structure in framing it, and at the same time it anchors the free-standing volume firmly back into the street plan.

Manhattan

To a certain degree Friedrichstadt can be compared to Manhattan; on the one hand it's plan is clearly legible amidst the sea of Berlin's buildings, and on the other hand, at least before the war, it had a similar density and business district character. In addition within Friedrichstadt has developed a type of city over time which, analogous to New York's gridiron plan, offers a dialectical conflict between the city plan and it's architecture. The architectural landscape has freed itself from the corset of the street grid. In this *third way*, as Manfredo Tafuri calls it, Friedrichstadt approaches a type of city where *the freedom, which is given to each architectural fragment, is embedded into a structure whose form is not determined by the individual fragment.*

Dialectical City

In particular since East Berlin is now *on the map* again, and exists in our minds as an integral part of the city centre, it becomes obvious that some individual buildings have developed a relationship above and independent to the grid of the streets. This transgressive dialogue (generated by the Wall) has become an integral part of Friedrichstadt, and should particularly be taken into account in the case of the GGZ.

Our proposal seeks to identify and continue the theme of the collage-like superimposition of historical architectural elements, and we regard the resulting urban figure as a direct result of the dialectic co-existence of a geometrical and a landscape order in this part of the city.

Historische Entwicklung der südlichen Friedrichstadt
Historical development of southern Friedrichstadt

Stadt der Toleranz
City of Tolerance

Barocke Synkopen
Baroque Syncopations

Das steinerne Berlin
The Stony Berlin

Kolonisierung der Ruinenlandschaft
Colonising the Landscape of Ruins

Die neue Stadt
The New City

Umorientierung der Territorien
Reversing the Territories

Retrospektive Stadtreparatur
Retrospective Urban Repair

Rückwirkende Integration
Retroactive Integration

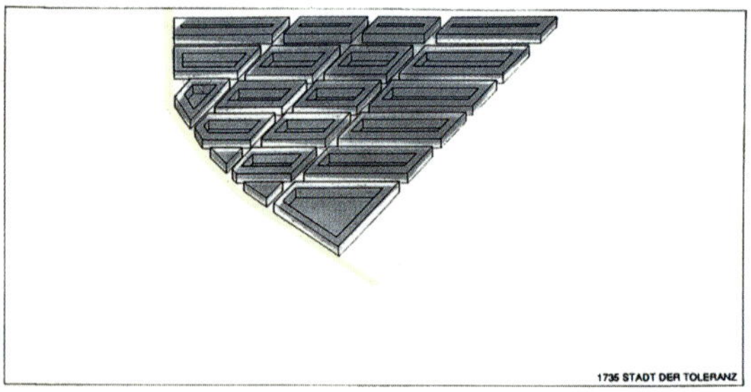

1735 STADT DER TOLERANZ

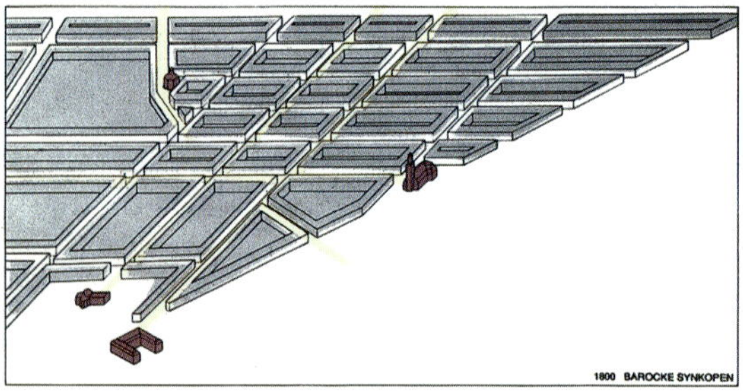

1800 BAROCKE SYNKOPEN

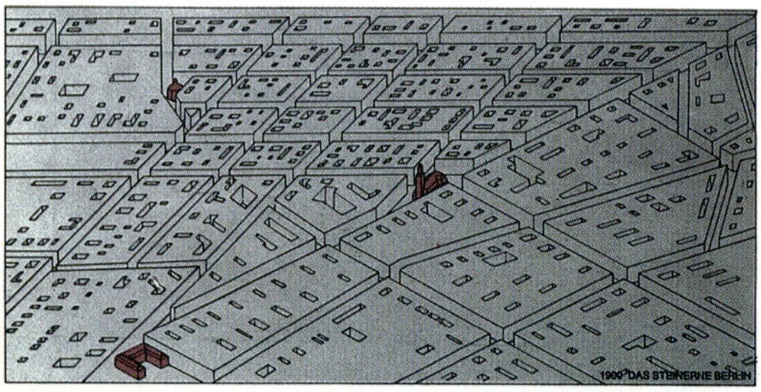

1900 DAS STEINERNE BERLIN

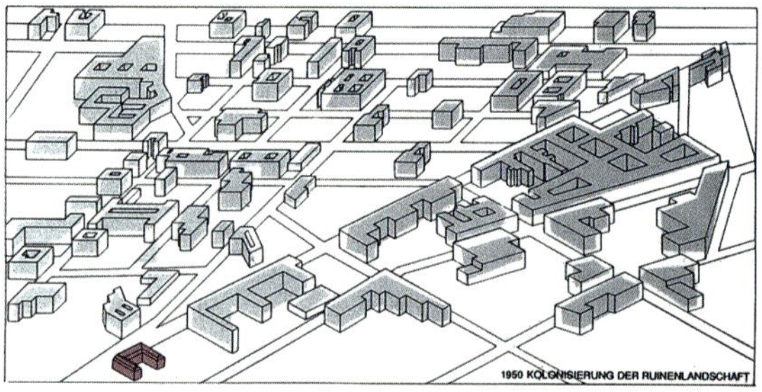

1950 KOLONISIERUNG DER RUINENLANDSCHAFT

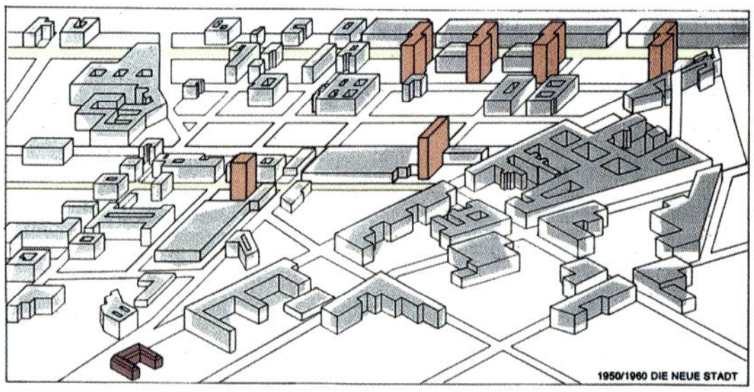

1950/1960 DIE NEUE STADT

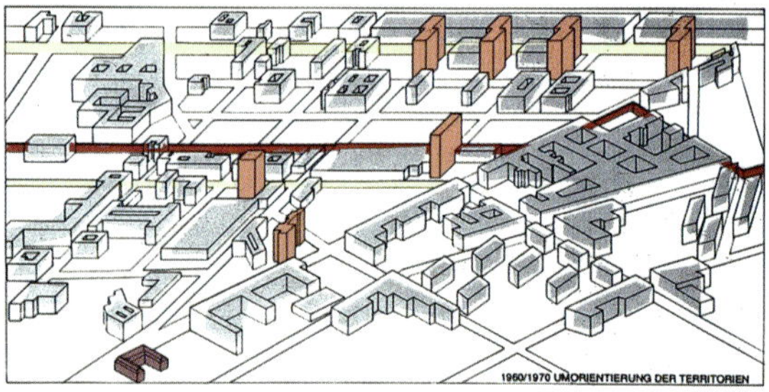

1960/1970 UMORIENTIERUNG DER TERRITORIEN

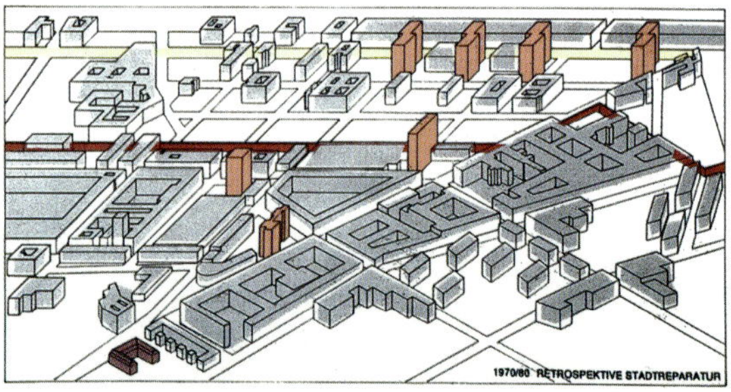

1970/80 RETROSPEKTIVE STADTREPARATUR

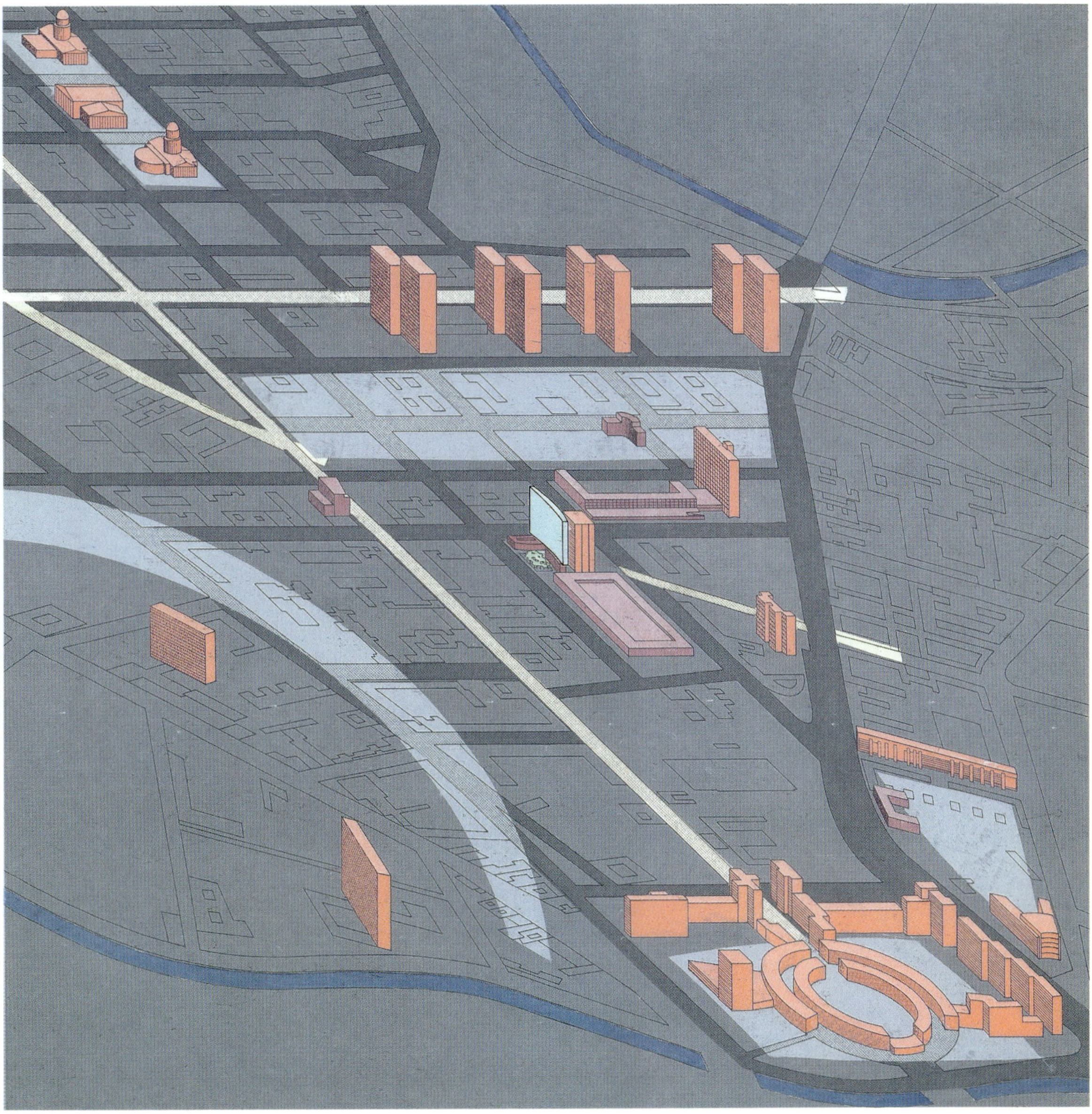

Perspektive *Dialog über die Mauer*
Perspective *Dialogue across the Wall*

Stadtgrundriss *Dialog über die Mauer*
Urban plan *Dialogue across the Wall*

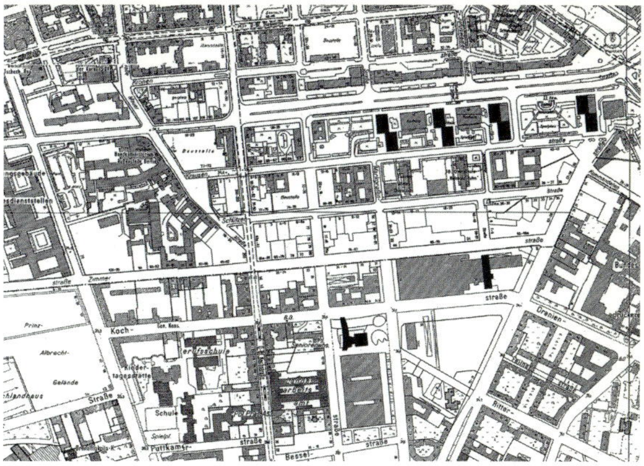
Kronen
Zimmer
straße
Prinz-
Albrecht-
Gelände
Koch-
Kinder-
tagesstätte
Schule
Spielpl.
Straße
Puttkamer-
straße
Bessel-
Oranien-
Ritter-
Bundes
Baustelle

Blick in die Kochstrasse Richtung Westen, Collage

View along Kochstrasse towards the west, collage

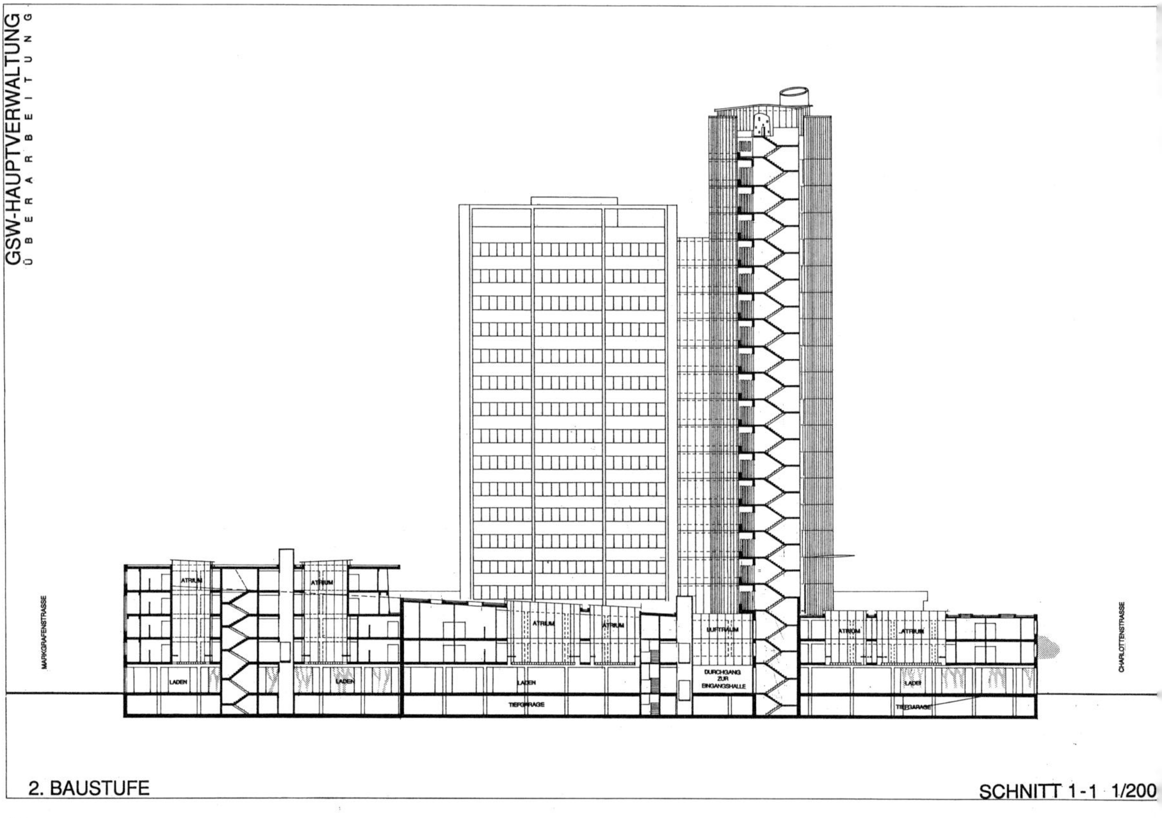

GSW-HAUPTVERWALTUNG
ÜBERARBEITUNG

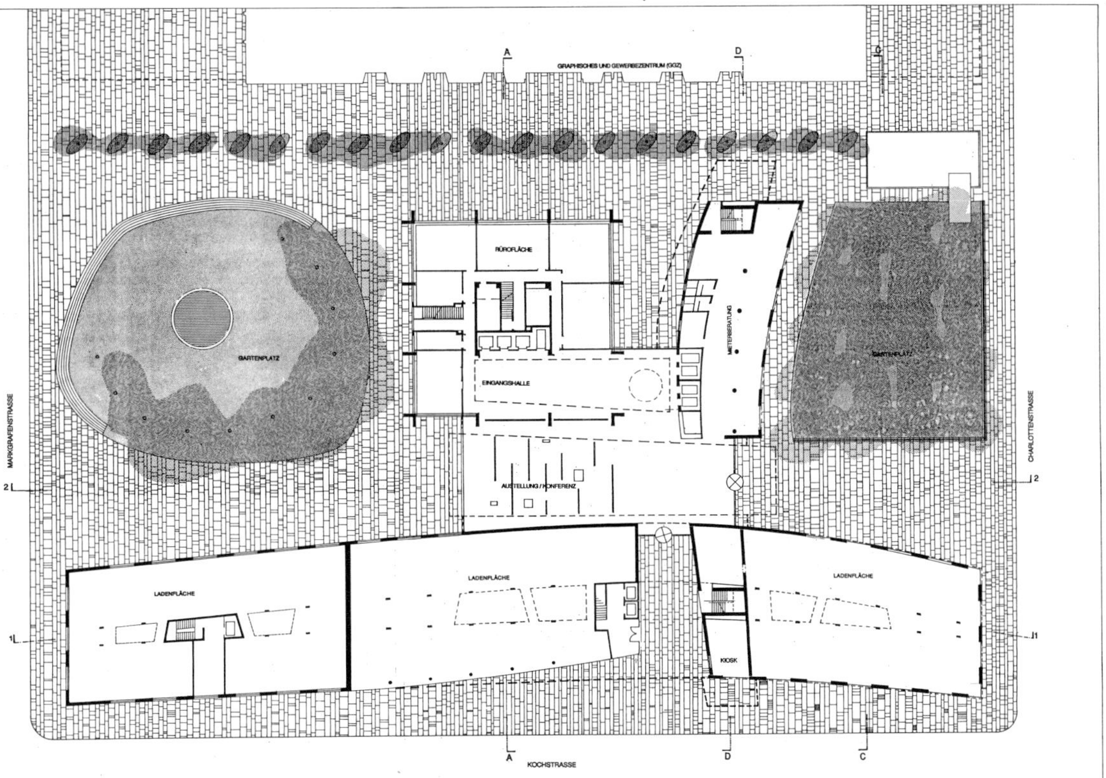

2. BAUSTUFE

ERDGESCHOSS 1/200

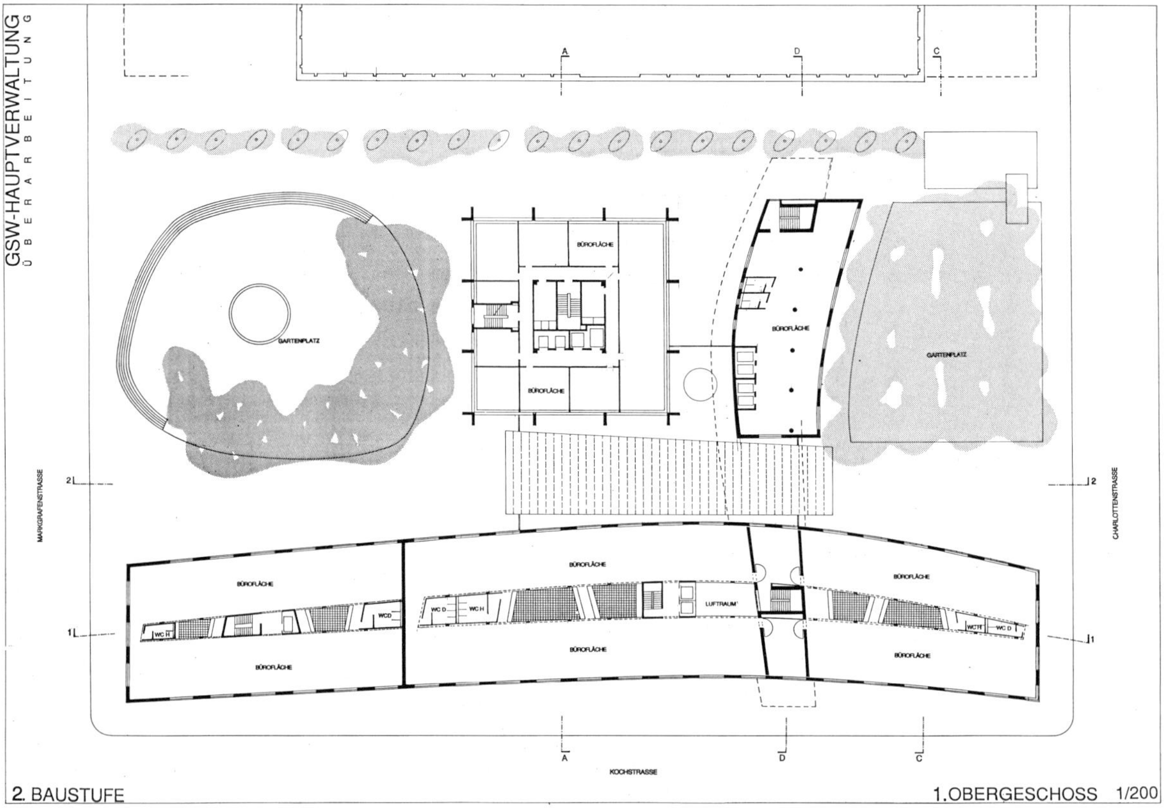
GSW-HAUPTVERWALTUNG
ÜBERARBEITUNG
GARTENPLATZ
BÜROFLÄCHE
BÜROFLÄCHE
BÜROFLÄCHE
GARTENPLATZ
MARKGRAFENSTRASSE
CHARLOTTENSTRASSE
BÜROFLÄCHE
BÜROFLÄCHE
BÜROFLÄCHE
WC H
WCD
WC D
WC H
LUFTRAUM
WC H
WC D
BÜROFLÄCHE
BÜROFLÄCHE
BÜROFLÄCHE
A
D
C
KOCHSTRASSE
2. BAUSTUFE
1.OBERGESCHOSS 1/200

AXEL SPRINGER VERLAG

Blick in die Kochstrasse Richtung Osten, Collage
View along Kochstrasse towards the east, collage

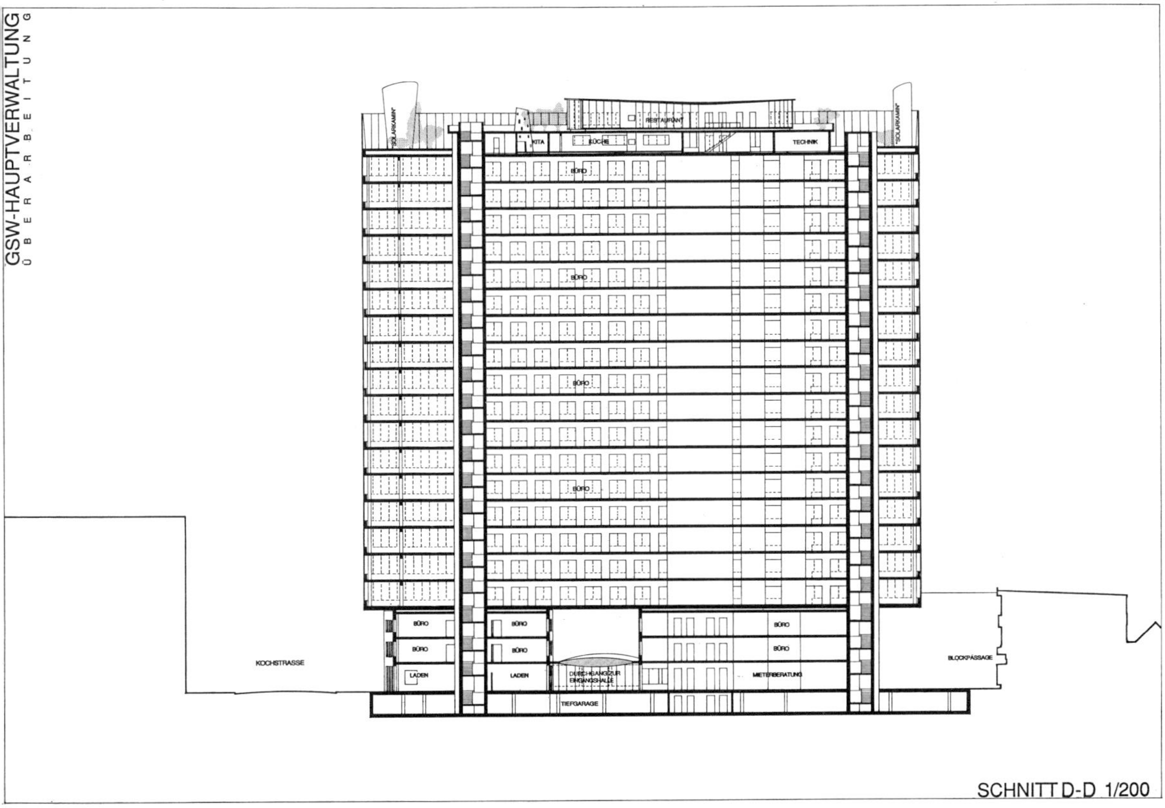

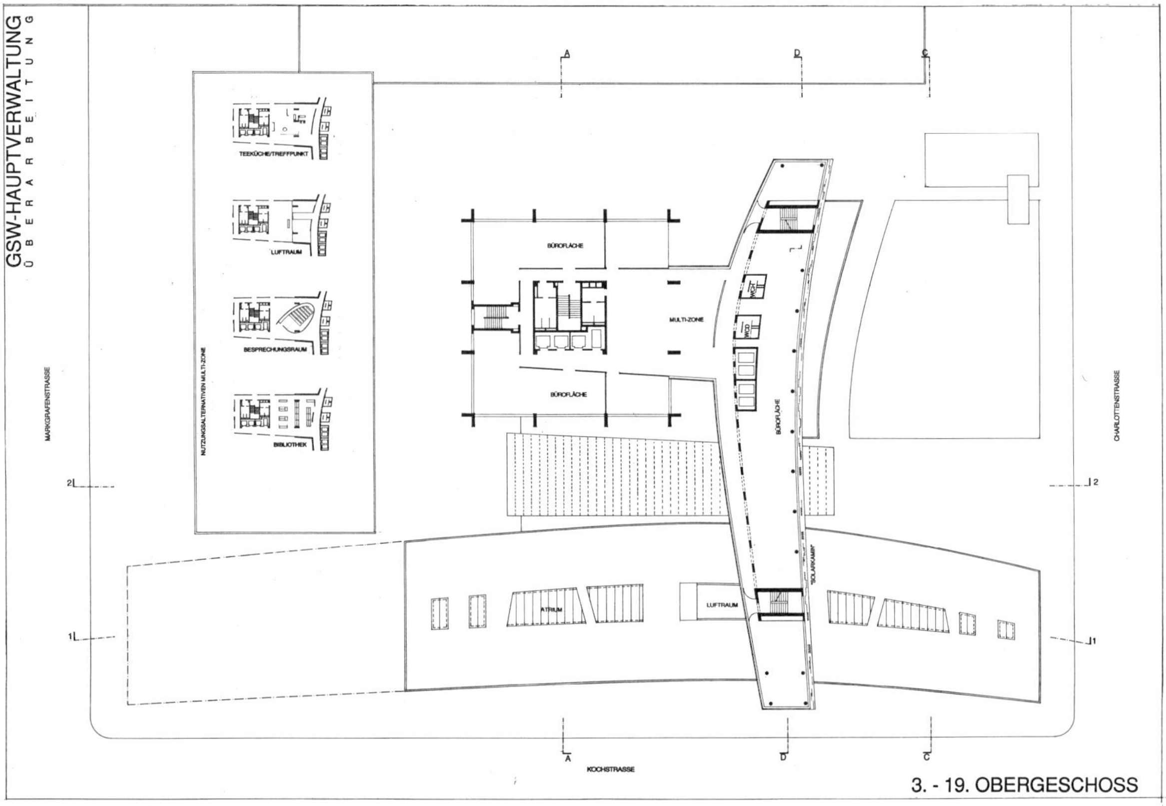

Blick vom bestehenden Hochhaus Richtung Norden
View from the existing tower towards the north

Isometrie zweite Baustufe
Second stage construction, isometric

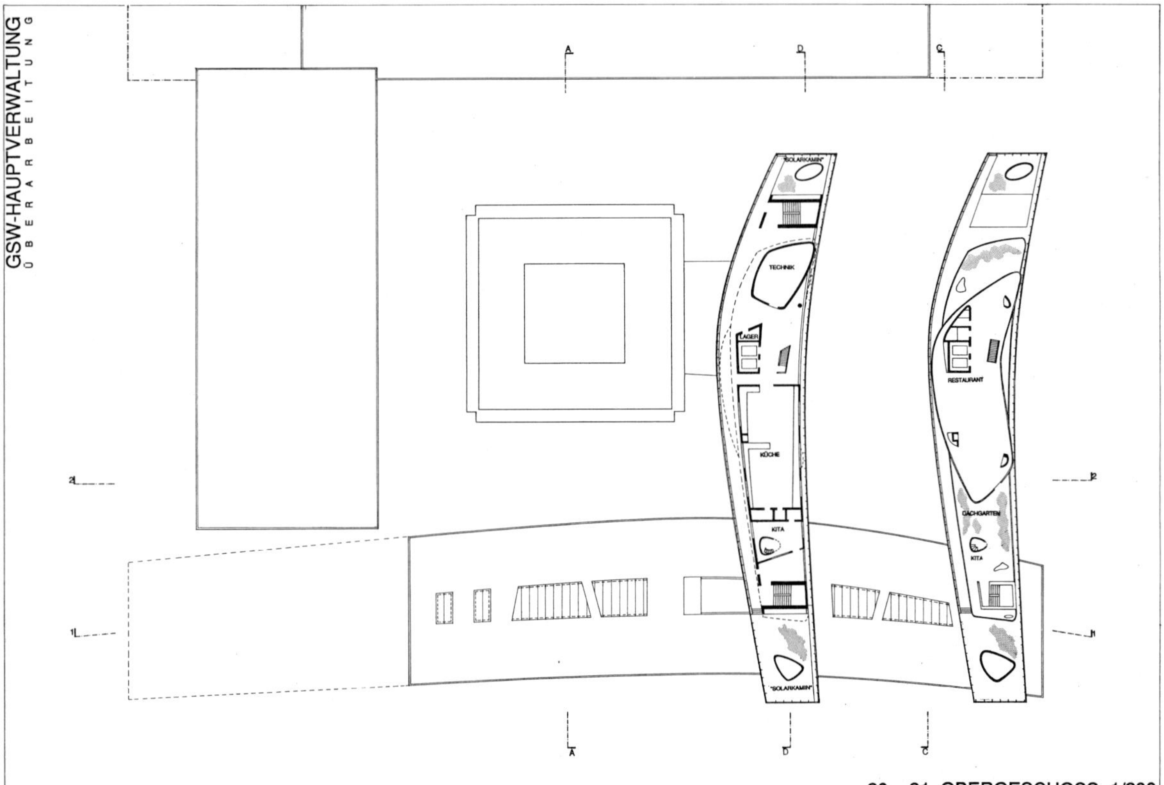

20. - 21. OBERGESCHOSS 1/200

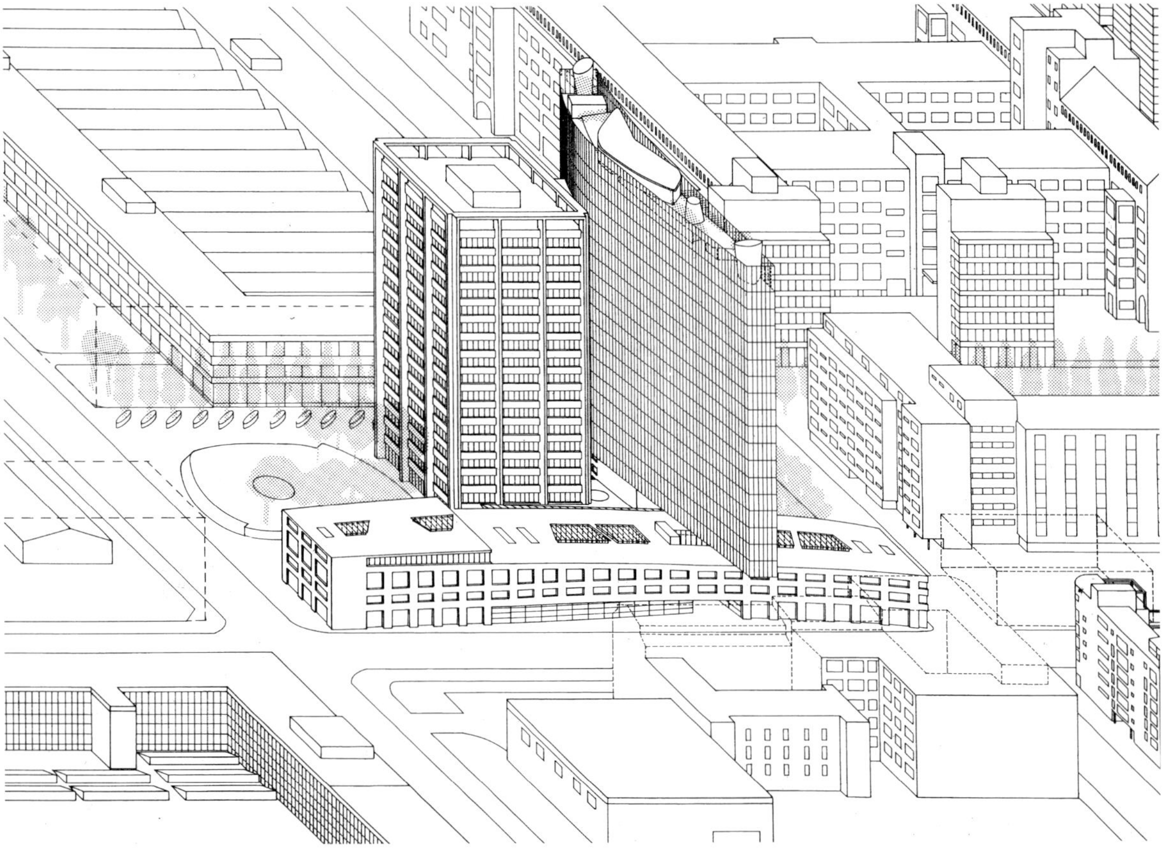

Innenperspektive mit Lüftungsprinzip
Interior perspective with ventilation (air flow) diagram

Die Reaktion auf Wind und Sonne
Response to wind and sun

Integration von Statik und Haustechnik, Axonometrie
Integration of structure and services, axonometric

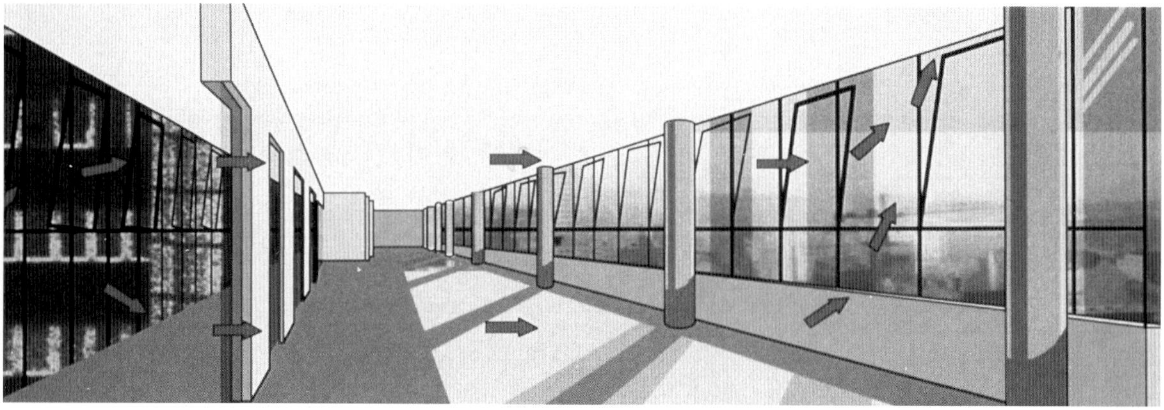

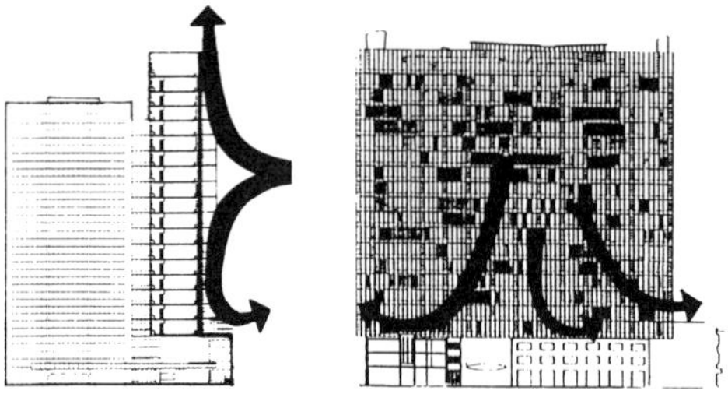

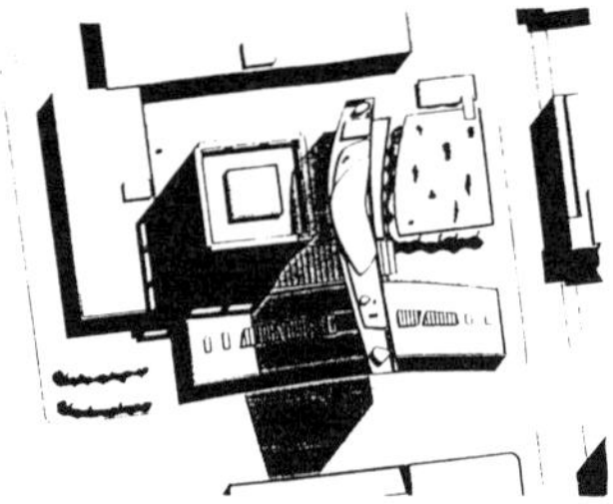

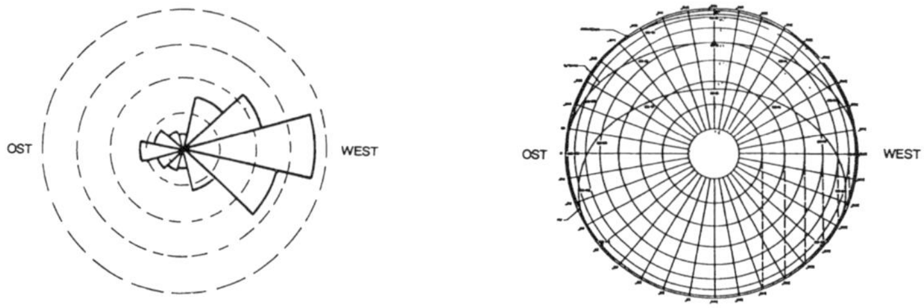

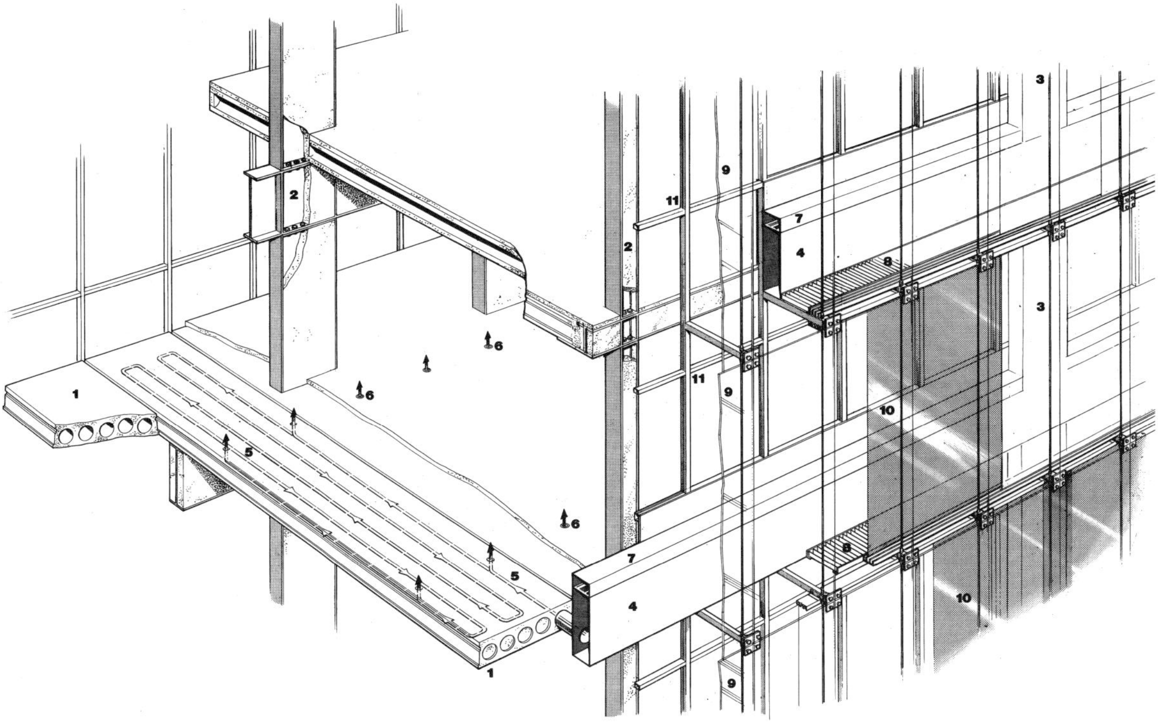

1 Vorgespannte Hohlbalkendecke
2 Stahlverbundstützen
3 Äussere Glashaut
4 Zuluftführung
5 Luftführung in der Rohdecke
6 Luftauslässe im Fussboden
7 Kabeltrasse für Elektro und Daten
8 Wartungsgang
9 Hängekonstruktion
10 Sonnenschutzläden
11 Innenfassade

1 Hollocore concrete slabs
2 Composite steel and concrete columns
3 Outer glass skin
4 Air duct
5 Ventilation through the concrete slab
6 Floor outlets for ventilation
7 Tray for electrical and data network cabling
8 Maintenance and cleaning gangway
9 Suspension cable construction
10 Solar shutters
11 Inner façade

Öffentlicher Raum

Das gesamte Grundstück wurde als eine kontinuierliche Fläche mit dem für Berliner Strassenräume typischen Mosaikpflaster aus schlesischem Granit belegt. Damit ist nicht nur die Grenze zwischen (privater) Grundstücksfläche und (öffentlichem) Gehsteig beinahe aufgehoben, sondern die gleichbleibende Textur des Pflasters begleitet den Fussgänger bis in das Gebäude hinein. Auf diesem Steinboden befinden sich *Teppiche,* die zum Verweilen einladen. Zur Markgrafenstrasse hin die *Bärentatze*, ein um ein paar Stufen erhöhter Hain mit Platanen, zur Charlottenstrasse der *Fliegende Teppich*, eine Holzterrasse mit Stufen und Bäumen. Das alte Hochhaus wird mit dem für die 50er-Jahre so typischen Betonwerksteinmaterial markiert und am Eingang zum Flachbau befindet sich eine Insel aus Granitplatten. Die Gebäudeformation schafft klar gefasste Aussenräume in allen vier Himmelsrichtungen: nach Süden eine baumbegleitete *Passage*, die die Markgrafen- und die Charlottenstrasse verbindet, nach Osten ein grüner Gartenplatz als Endpunkt eines im Verlauf der ehemaligen Junkerstrasse geplanten *Pocket Parks*, im Westen eine Caféterrasse. An der Kochstrasse führt der sanfte Schwung der Strassenfassade den Fussgänger in den Gebäudekomplex hinein und bietet gleichzeitig grosszügigen Raum für eine Bushaltestelle der Berliner Verkehrsbetriebe.

Public Space

The whole site is treated as a single field and is covered with Berlin's typical pavement material (granite sets). In this way the limits between (public) pavement and (private) site have been virtually eliminated, and the continuous surface leads one right into the entrance hall.
On this granite floor a number of *mats* mark out significant places. Towards Markgrafenstrasse there is the so-called *bear's paw*, a raised grove of plane-trees; towards Charlottenstrasse lies the timber terrace of the *flying carpet*; around the existing high-rise building there is a mat of (typically 1950s) terrazzo and at the entrance into the low-rise *baguette* there is an island of granite slabs.
The composition of building volumes creates clearly defined exterior spaces in all four directions. To the south there is a tree-lined passage connecting Markgrafenstrasse and Charlottenstrasse. To the east a green square forms an end to a *pocket park* in the line of the former *Junkerstrasse*, and to the west there is a generous terrace for the café. Along Kochstrasse the building gently recedes in a long curve to extend the space of the street. At its widest point the pavement offers entry into the building and allows room for people waiting at the bus stop.

P
Frei

AXEL SPRINGER VERLAG

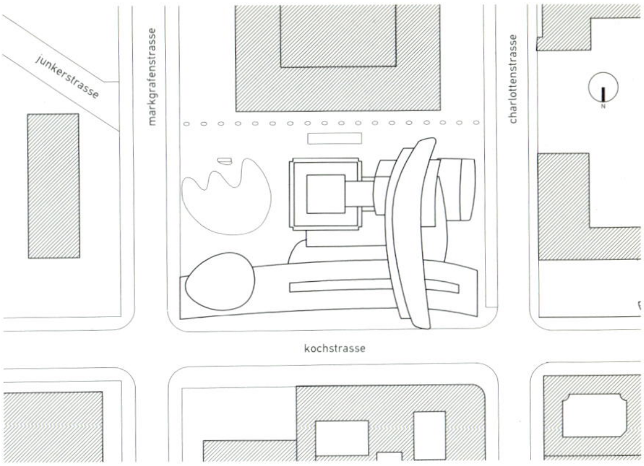

Der Ruheplatz der Göttin Pele Skulptur von Klaus Noculak
***The resting place of the goddess Pele* sculpture by Klaus Noculak**

Lageplan
Site plan

Aussenraumkonzept
Landscaping concept

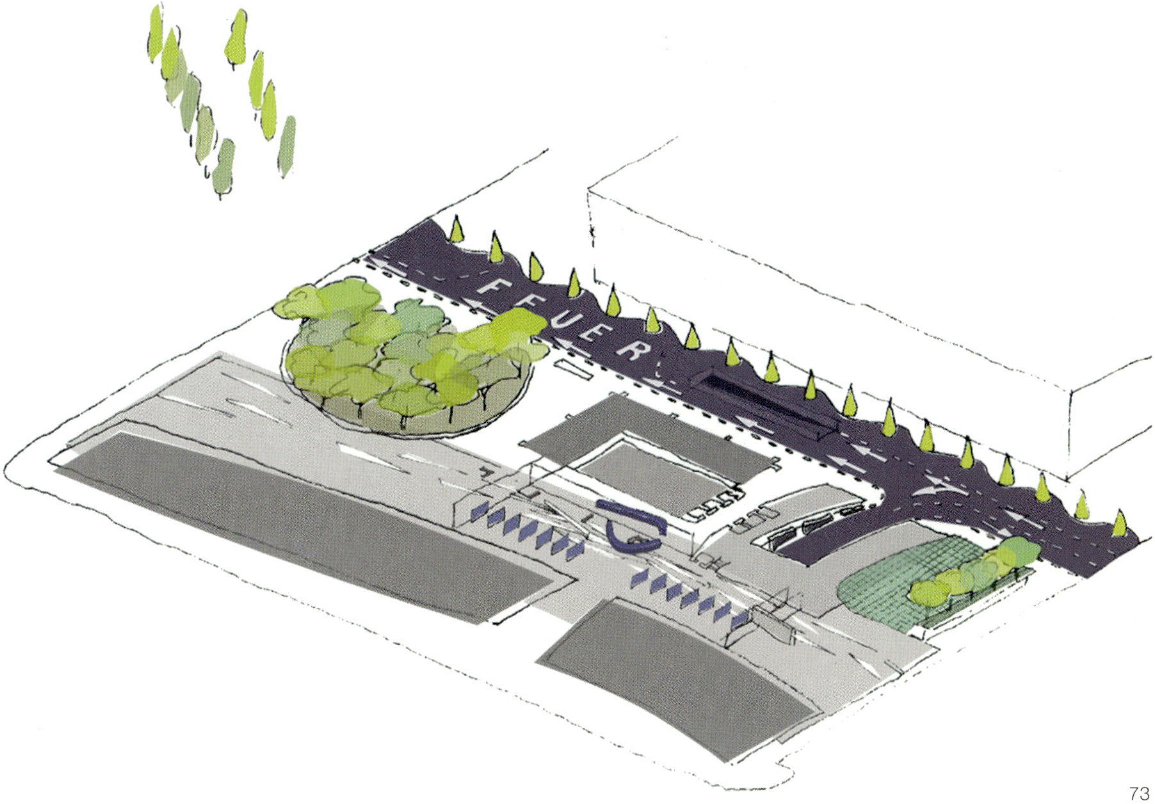

Längsschnitt durch das mechanische Parksystem und Pillbox

Long section through mechanical parking system and pillbox

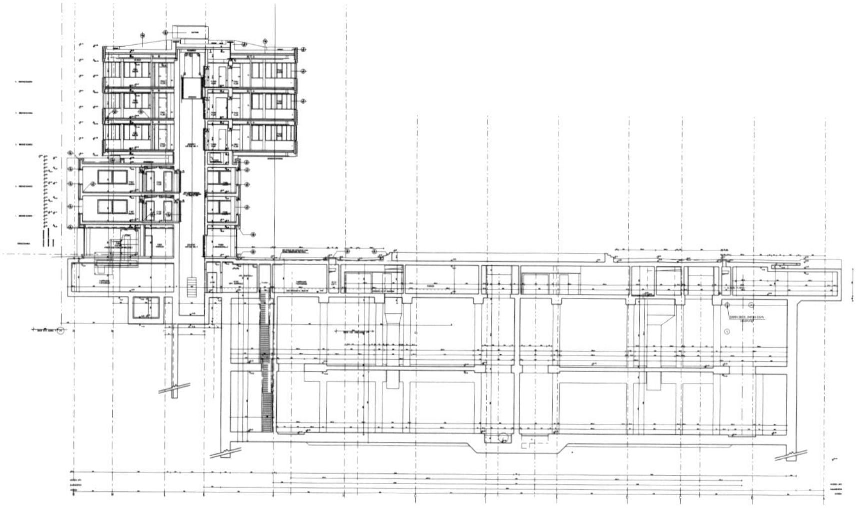

Grundriss 1. Untergeschoss M. ca. 1:750

Basement plan scale ca. 1:750

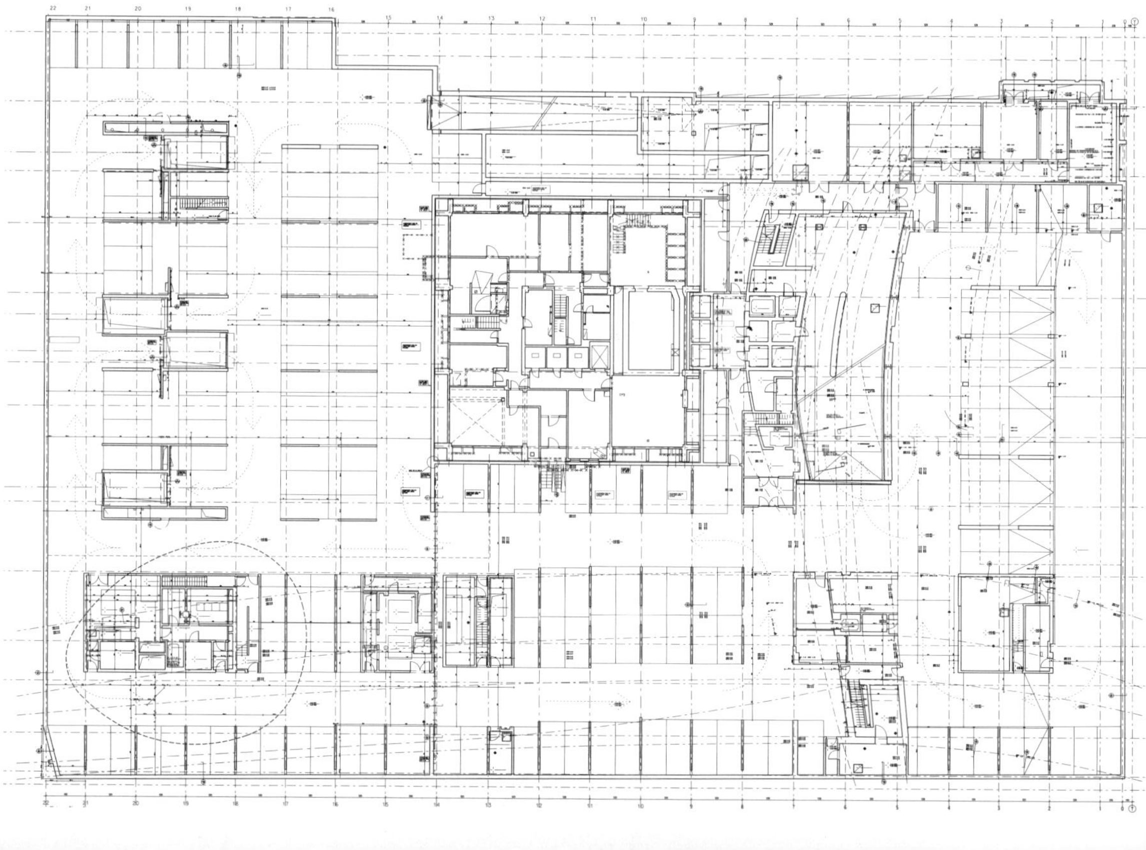

Mechanisches Parken

Auf Grund der ungünstigen Grundwasserverhältnisse und der daraus folgenden hohen Gründungskosten für eventuelle Tiefgeschosse wurde in der GSW Hauptverwaltung ein mechanisches Tiefparksystem eingebaut.
Die Anlage besteht aus vier unabhängigen Parksystemen, die zusammen Platz für 224 Fahrzeuge bieten. Jedes dieser Systeme hat zwei Vertikalförderer und sechs Parkebenen, die aus Einzelplatzmodulen auf Rollenbahnen bestehen.
Der Zugang erfolgt über vier Einfahrtsräume mit jeweils zwei Rolltoren im 1. Untergeschoss.
Nach der Einfahrt in einen dieser Räume werden Fahrzeuge vollautomatisch durch die Anlage gelagert und auf Wunsch wieder ausgeliefert. Pro Stunde können so ca. 100–120 Fahrzeuge ein- und ausgeparkt werden.

Mechanical parking

Due to the high level of ground water on the site and the necessary expense involved in waterproofing the underground floors, it was decided to equip the GSW Headquarters building with a mechanical parking system.
This system consists of four independent machines offering a total of 224 car parking spaces. Each machine has two vertical lifts and six levels consisting of single car-pods on horizontal belts. The system is accessed through four cabins in the basement floor.
After driving into one of this cabins, cars are stored away automatically and are collected on demand. Around 100–120 cars per hour can be delivered into or retrieved from the system.

Grundriss Einfahrtskabine

Drive-in platform for parking system, plan

Detail Schnitt mechanisches Parksystem

Section detail of the mechanical parking system

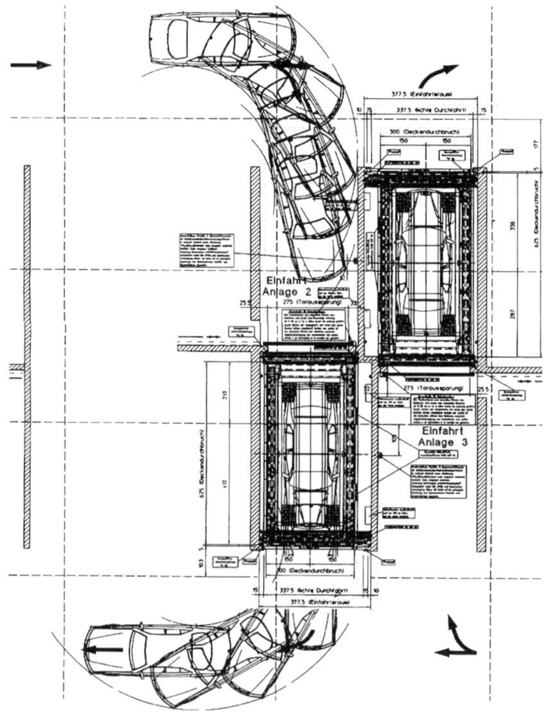

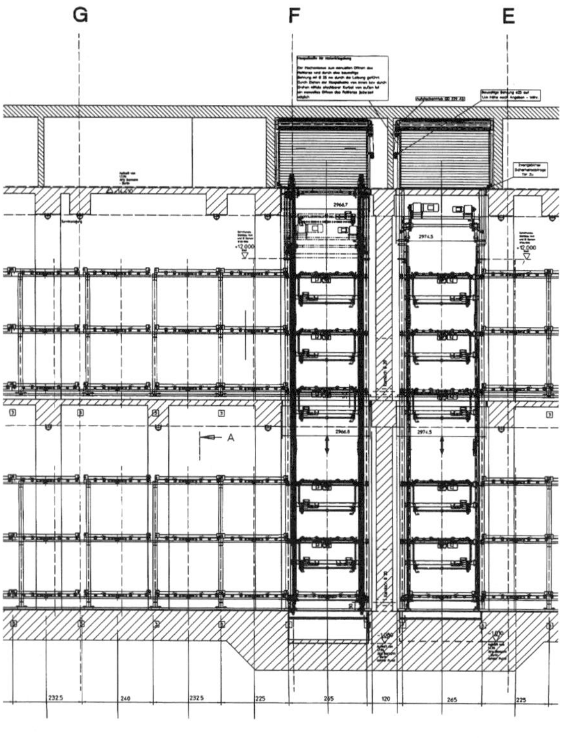

Eingangshalle

Die Eingangshalle ist als überdachter Strassenraum konzipiert. Sie ist der öffentliche Ort des Hauses, von dem aus die Gebäudeteile einzeln identifizierbar und zugänglich sind. Darüber hinaus bietet sie Raum für Ausstellungen und andere Veranstaltungen; mit demontierbaren Stellwänden und einem ausfahrbaren Vorhang kann die Fläche unterteilt werden.
Die Halle ist 800 m^2 gross und nur 2,80 m hoch. Ihr flacher Raum steht im klaren Kontrast zur aufstrebenden Vertikalität der Hochhäuser. Das Tageslicht ist gedämpft, das Auge wird auf die Dächer gelenkt, die von zwei Seiten auskragen. Die eine Hälfte ist flach, die andere – geschwungen wie eine Welle – dient als Reflektor für ruhiges Nordlicht, das durch ein langgestrecktes Dachfenster einfällt. Der Blick wandert dann horizontal entlang zweier sich kreuzender Achsen zu den Aussenräumen: die Strasse, der Grünplatz, die Passage und die Terrasse.
Am zentralen Punkt der Halle, von allen Seiten einsehbar, leuchtet blau der Tresen der Reception.
Begibt man sich von dort in den Flachbau, betritt man den ca. 10 m hohen, tagesbelichteten Raum des Atriums. Entscheidet man sich für Turm oder Scheibe, passiert man ein Oberlicht, das wie eine Zoom-Linse auf die Hochhäuser gerichtet ist.
Man verlässt den flachen Eingangsraum in einer Liftkabine, um dann (nach der Fahrt nach oben) in einem der Obergeschosse einen vollverglasten Vorraum zu betreten, der mit dem Blick über die Stadt ein Gefühl befreiender Weite und Grosszügigkeit vermittelt.

Entrance Hall

The entrance hall was conceived as a covered street. It is the public space from which all parts of the building can be identified and entered. In addition it provides opportunity for exhibitions and other events – demountable screens and a retractable curtain can modify the space.
The hall is ca. 800 sqm in extent and only 2.8 m high. It's horizontality is in clear contrast to the verticality of the high-rise buildings. The level of daylight is lowered – one's eye wanders to the two ceilings which seem to be cantilevering from the opposing buildings. One of these ceilings is horizontal, whilst the other forms a wave which acts as a reflector for north light filtering into the hall through a long clerestory. One's view is then lead to the external spaces which anchor two crossing axes: the street, the garden, the passage and the terrace.
In the centre – visible from everywhere – is the luminous blue reception desk.
If from here you want to go to the low-rise *baguette* you will enter the long, ca. 10 m high, day-lit space of the *atrium*.
If, however, you want to go to the high-rise buildings you will pass beneath a circular roof-light, which is directed towards the ascending cluster of vertical elements like a zoom lens. One leaves the ground floor in a lift cabin to enter the high-rise through a fully glazed lift lobby which – with its views across the city – offers liberating openness and generosity.

Studie Eingangshalle von Westen
Sketch of the entrance hall from the west

Grundriss Erdgeschoss M. ca. 1:1000
Ground floor plan scale ca. 1:1000

Studie Eingangshalle von Osten
Sketch of entrance hall from the east

Studie Eingangshalle von Norden
Sketch of the entrance hall from the north

Flachbau (Baguette)

Das Baguette ist als Strassengebäude für Läden (im Erdgeschoss) und Gewerbe (im 1. und 2. Obergeschoss) geplant worden. Eine zweigeschossige, tagesbelichtete, interne *Strasse* von der aus die Büroflächen betreten werden, gibt ihm auch im Innern öffentlichen Charakter.
Dieses sogenannte *Atrium* ist ein insgesamt 100 m langer und 6 m breiter, leicht geschwungener Raum, der als Überlagerung zweier Teilräume gedacht ist: Die äusseren Längswände aus Sichtbeton, in die eine lange Reihe von Mattglastüren eingelassen ist, beschreiben einen *Nachtraum*; denn diese Flächen werden bei Nacht angestrahlt. Das Tageslicht reflektiert im Verlauf des ca. 75 m langen Oberlichtbandes an hellen Brüstungen bis in das Erdgeschoss hinab, um einen in den *Nachtraum* eingeschriebenen *Tagraum* zu definieren. So nimmt der Querschnitt des Atriums je nach Tageszeit einen anderen Charakter an.
Schon in der Eingangszone an der Kochstrasse und in dem ganzen Atrium ist man der Hochhausscheibe über dem Baguette gewahr, deren *Fussabdruck* als Schatten sichtbar ist. Sowohl vom Ost- wie vom Westende des Atriums sieht man dann auch ihre Fassaden, die sich über dem langen horizontalen Körper des Flachbaus erheben.

Baguette (low-rise building)

The *baguette* was designed as a *street-building* for shops (on the ground floor) and offices (on the first and second floors). The double-storey, daylit internal street for access to the office areas gives the building its public character.
This so called *atrium* is a 100 m long, 6 m wide, slightly curved space. It was conceived in terms of the superimposition of two spaces: a wide *night-space* into which is set a narrower *day-space*. The night-space is defined by the outer walls with their long rows of office doors whose fair-faced concrete surfaces are illuminated at night. The day-space is the narrower (and taller) 2 m wide slice of space defined by natural light. This washes down from the 75 m long roof-light over plastered bands to reach the ground floor. In this way the atrium acquires a different spatial profile according to the time of day.
Already in the entrance zone at Kochstrasse and along the whole atrium one is aware of the high-rise which leaves its *footprint* as a shadow on the roof-light. From both the western and the eastern ends of the atrium one is able to see it's façades as they hover over the long horizontal space.

GSW
ZÜBLIN
H

Charlottenstr.

Markgrafenstraße
Kochstraße
Sparkass

Sparkasse

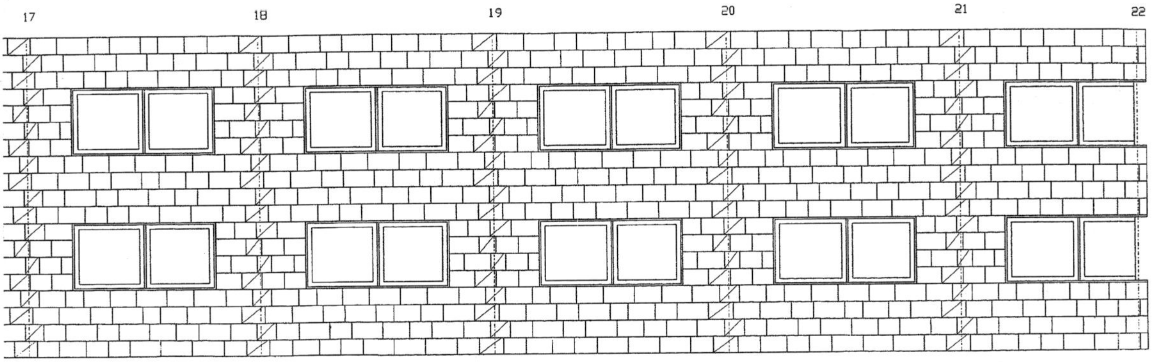

Flachbaufassade

Die Fassade des Flachbaus ist analog zu seiner liegenden, massiven Gebäudeform in einem schweren Material ausgeführt. Terrakottaplatten in einer grafitfarbigen Glasur wurden speziell für dieses Bauvorhaben entwickelt und angefertigt. Im Gegensatz zur leichten und *diffusen* Gestalt des aufstrebenden Hochhauses bietet dieser Bauteil das Bild eines kompakten, dem Boden verbundenen Baukörpers, der aber auf der Ostseite durch den Glaseinschub der Schaufensterfassaden vom Erdboden getrennt ist.
Da die Dimensionen der Fassade auf Grund des Gebäudegrundrisses von Fensterfeld zu Fensterfeld leicht variieren, beruht das Fugenbild der Keramikfassade nicht auf einem einheitlichen Raster. Statt dessen wurde zwischen gleichen Fassadenfeldern eine Plattenreihe angeordnet, die dem Baustellenmass angepasst werden kann.
Die horizontalen Fugen der Plattenfassade sind ca. 10 mm hoch, wobei hier die Glasur über die Ecke gezogen wurde und somit die unebene Kante aus dem Herstellungsprozess der Platten sichtbar bleibt. Die vertikalen Fugen sind im Gegensatz dazu geschnitten und deshalb nur 3 mm breit, sodass ein horizontales Fugenbild und ein lebendiger Rhythmus entstehen.

Low-rise façade

The low-rise building is clad with a solid and heavy material analogous to the mass of its horizontal volume. The terracotta tiles with their graphite coloured glazing were especially developed for this project. As opposed to the light and *diffused* character of the high-rise, the *baguette* appears to be a compact body, which is ground-related – except that its eastern end has been lifted up by the insertion of the glazed slice of the shops.
The dimensions of the interstitial spaces between windows vary due to the curve of the plan – so the widths of the terracotta tiles are not consistent. Instead there is one vertical row of tiles within every bay which has been adapted to site dimensions.
The horizontal joints between the tiles are 10 mm high, and exhibit a soft unevenness which is a result of the glaze having run over the edge during manufacture. The vertical joints – by contrast – are clean cut and only 3 mm wide, so that a pattern with horizontal emphasis and a lively vertical rhythm appears.

Ausschnitt Verlegeplan Südfassade
Partial coordination plan for the south façade

Typisches Eckdetail
Typical corner detail

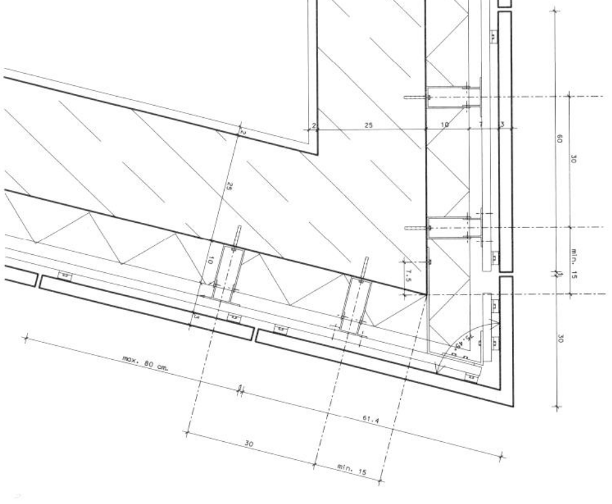

Schnitt Atrium M. ca. 1:1000
Section atrium scale ca. 1:1000

Studie Atrium
Sketch atrium

Grundriss 1. Obergeschoss M. ca. 1:1000
First floor plan scale ca. 1:1000

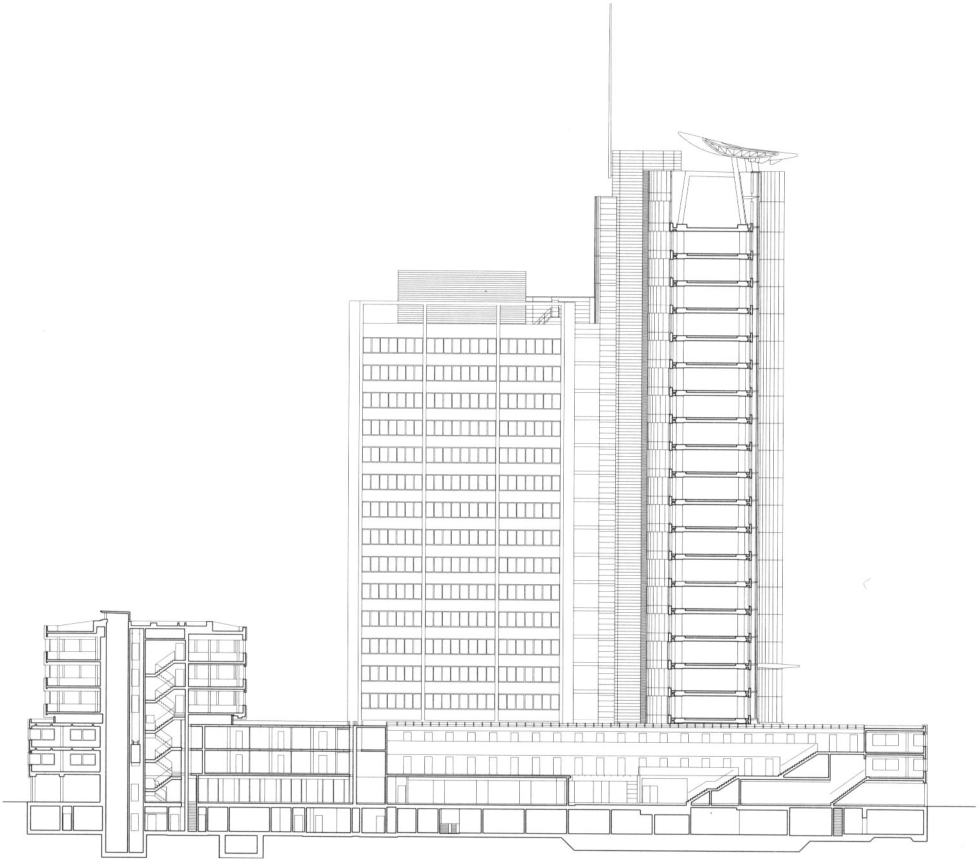

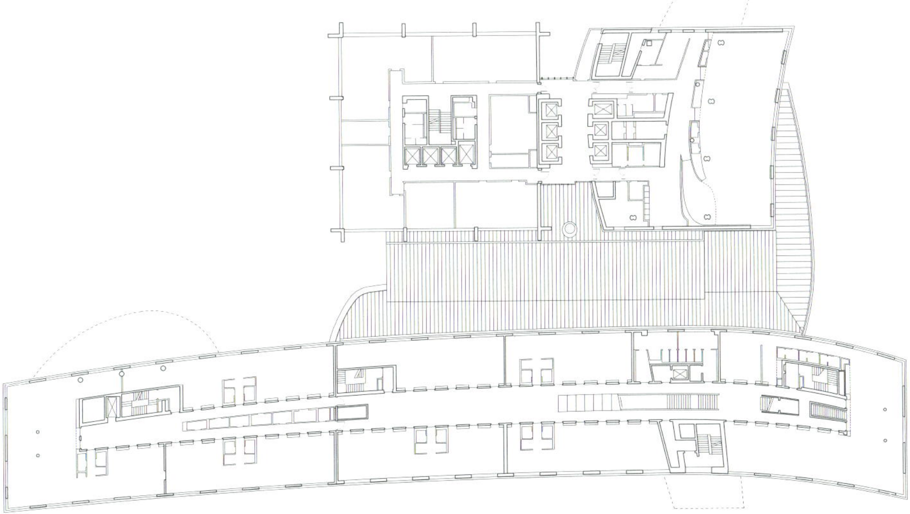

Innenaufnahme Atriummodell
Interior view of the atrium model

Atriummodell
Atrium model

Querschnitt *Tag- und Nachtraum*
Cross section *day- and night-space*

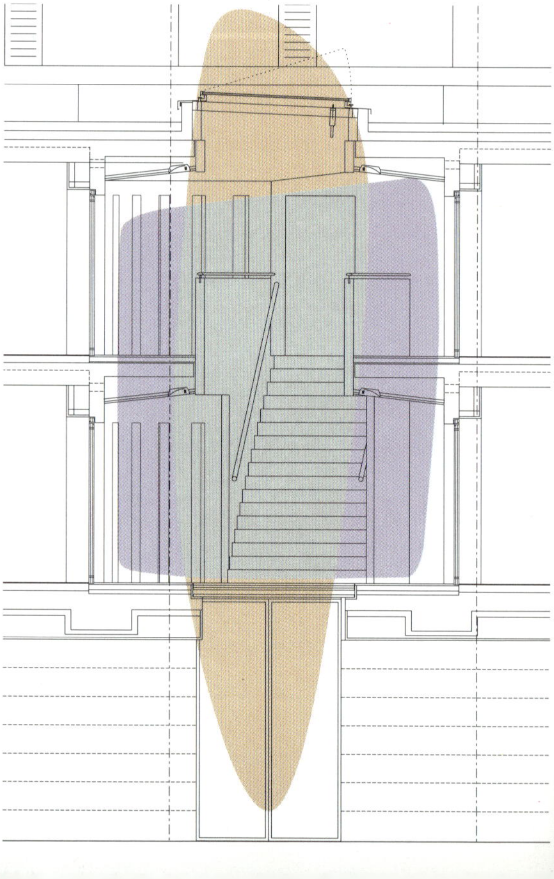

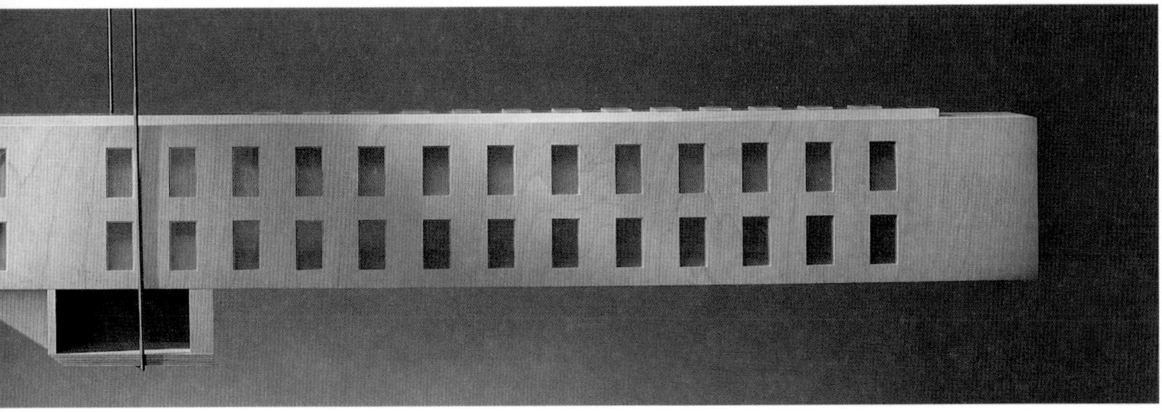

Baguettini

Das *Baguettini* enthält im Erdgeschoss eine Bar/Café mit grosszügiger Cafeterrasse und im 1.OG das Konferenzzentrum des Gebäudekomplexes.
Der Zugang zu diesen Konferenzräumen erfolgt vom Aufzugsvorraum über eine teils zweigeschossige, eher introvertierte Foyerzone mit Garderobe. Betritt man von dort das Konferenzzentrum, eröffnet sich eine andere Welt. Die grosszügige Höhe des Raums, die umlaufende Holzverkleidung der Wände mit grossformatigen Fenstern nach Westen und nicht zuletzt die Leuchtfelder in der Decke machen diesen Bereich zu einem speziellen Erlebnis.
Der 220 m^2 grosse Saal lässt sich in drei Räume unterteilen und ist mit vollständiger Konferenztechnik ausgestattet, die jedoch zunächst versteckt bleibt. Sowohl die Trennwände, die Multimediaausstattung als auch die Licht- und Lufttechnik sind in der sogenannten *Wunderwand* untergebracht und können je nach Bedarf über ein Touchpanel aktiviert werden.
Eiförmige Deckenschalen dienen zur indirekten Beleuchtung. Der Konferenzbereich ist sowohl in Ausrichtung wie Erschliessung dem Erdgeschoss zugeordnet und steht dem gesamten Gebäude zur Nutzung zur Verfügung.

Baguettini

The *baguettini* is a small building similar in height to the baguette, which is set back from the street so that its ground floor café can enjoy a generous west-facing terrace.
The main conference centre of the ensemble is on the first floor. Access to these conference rooms is from the lift lobby through a partially double-storey, introverted foyer-zone with cloakrooms.
On entering the conference rooms a different world is revealed: the generous ceiling height, the timber-panelled walls with large windows to the west, and not least the luminous egg-shaped dishes in the ceilings give these spaces special character.
The centre, 220 sqm in size, can be used either as one large room or it can be divided into three. It is equipped with complete (but invisible) conference technology: all the dividing walls, the AV-systems together with the light and ventilation equipment are hidden in the so-called *wonder wall* – from where the various elements can be activated through remote touch panels.
The dishes in the ceiling act as light reflectors for indirect lighting. The conference centre is deliberately situated with easy access from the ground floor, as it is to serve all occupants of the ensemble.

Explosionsaxonometrie Konferenzausstattung
Exploded axonometric for conference room equipment

Oberlichterschalen im Bau
Ceiling lightshells under construction

Wandverkleidung im Bau
Wall paneling under construction

Deckenspiegel M. ca. 1:330
Reflected ceiling plan scale ca. 1:330

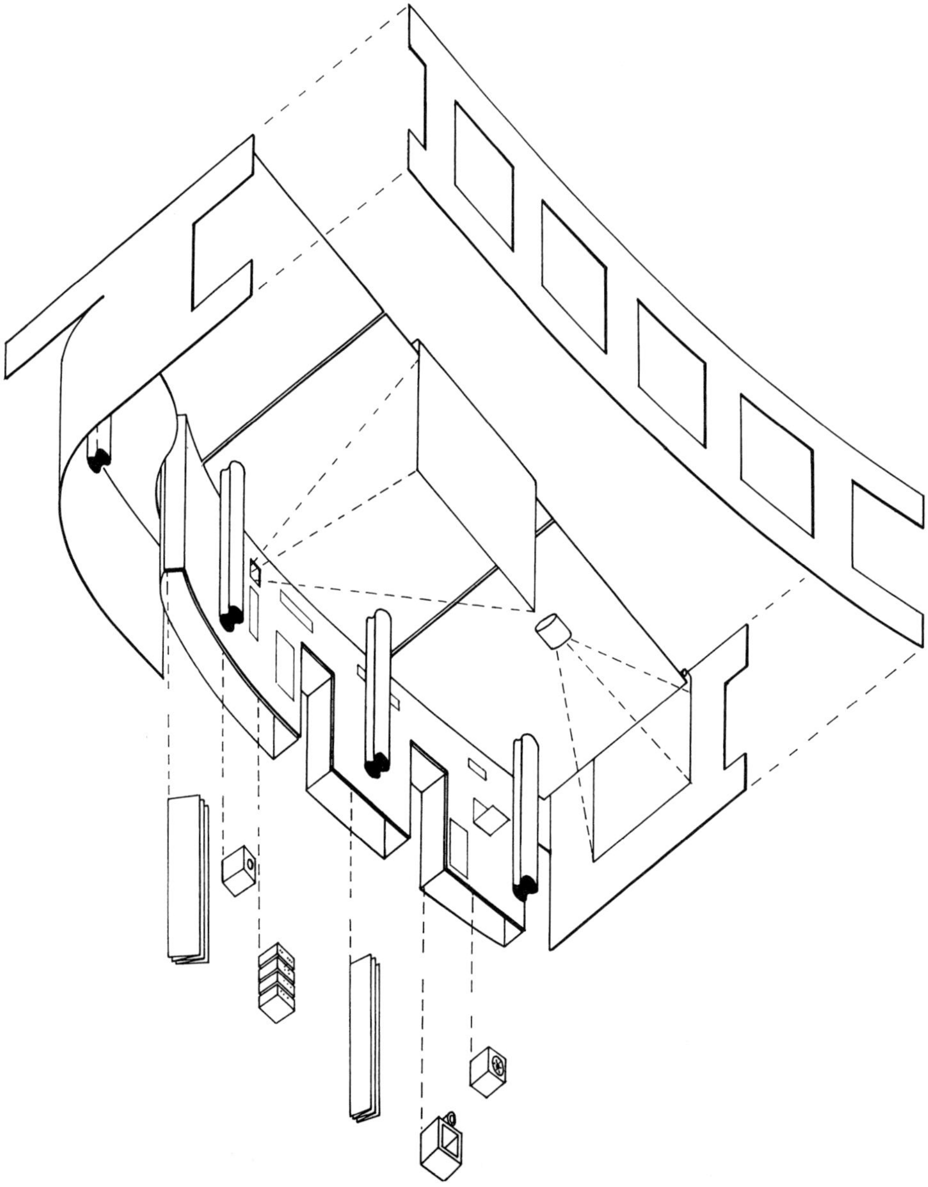

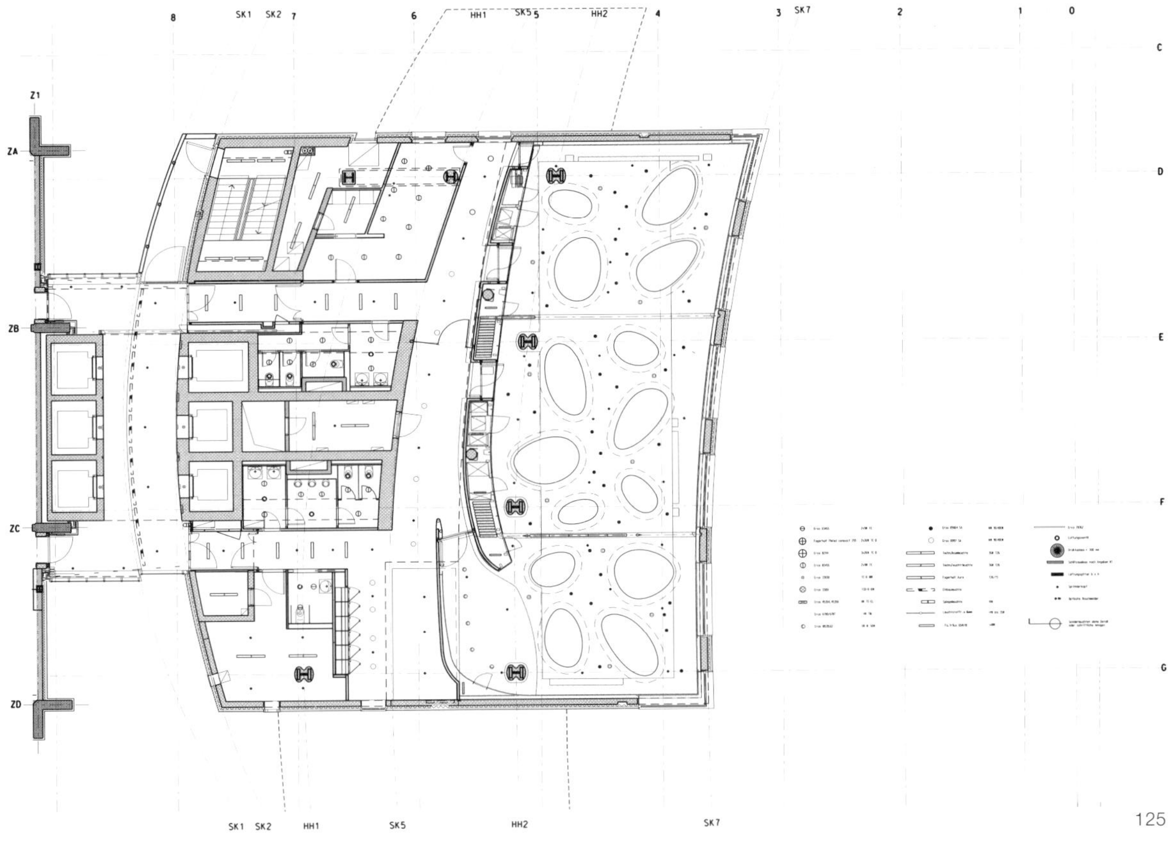
8
SK1 SK2 7
6
HH1
SK5 5
HH2
4
3 SK7
2
1
0
C
D
E
F
G
Z1
ZA
ZB
ZC
ZD
SK1 SK2
HH1
SK5
HH2
SK7

Pillbox

Dieser Bauteil entstand zunächst aus dem städtebaulichen Ansatz der Betonung der Strassenecke. Er ist jedoch ein vieldeutiger Körper: Die Rundform, aus mehreren Radien zusammengesetzt, verändert ihren Charakter, je nachdem aus welcher Richtung man sie betrachtet. Seine vielfarbige Haut unterstützt den Eindruck eines sich nach verschiedenen Seiten verändernden Objektes. Während sie von Norden gesehen fett und lastend auf dem Dach des Flachbaus aufliegt, balanciert sie von Süden und Osten gesehen prekär auf der Kante, scheinbar im Widerspruch zur Schwerkraft.

Der Bauteil ist auch als Konstruktion interessant. Er besteht aus einem dreigeschossigen Stahlverbundsystem, das von einem ca. 2 m hohen Stahlträgerrost abhängt, der auf einem zentralen sechsgeschossigen Betonkern aufliegt.

Pillbox

This ambiguous volume was developed out of the desire to emphasize the street corner. With its round figure constructed from a number of radii, the appearance of the *pillbox* depends on the position of the viewer. Its multi-coloured skin supports the impression of a continuously changing object. Looking fat and heavy from the north, when seen from the east or south it balances precariously on the building edge, seemingly defying gravity.

The building is also interesting from a structural point of view. Its three floor plates are suspended from 2 m high steel girders which rest on a six-storeyed central concrete core.

ZÜBLIN
TABAKPOINT

BUS

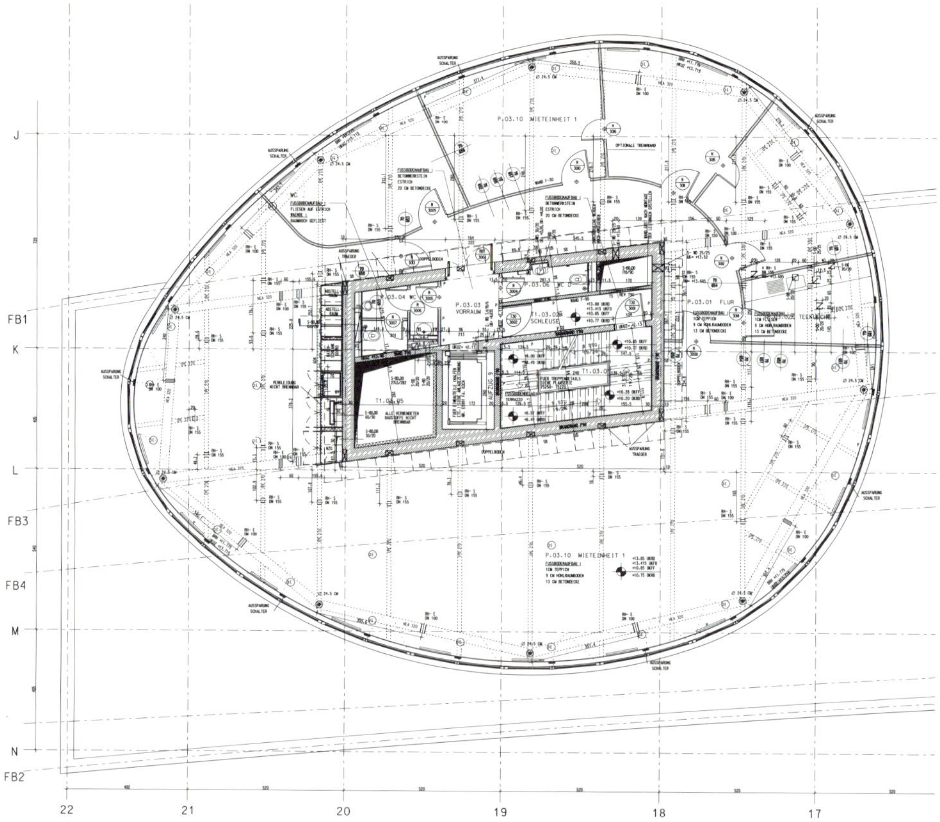

Grundriss Pillbox M. ca. 1:250
Plan of the pillbox scale ca. 1:250

Montage Trägerrost
Installation of the main girders

Stahlträgerrost für Hängekonstruktion
Cantilevering steel girders for the suspended floor construction

AXEL SPRINGER

Knotenbleche der Stahlkonstruktion
Gusset plates for the steel girder floor construction

Hängestützen
Suspension columns

Montage Betonverbunddecken
Installation of composite floor

Detail der Hängekonstruktion
Detail of the suspended steel construction

Vollendeter Rohbau
Assembled composite structure

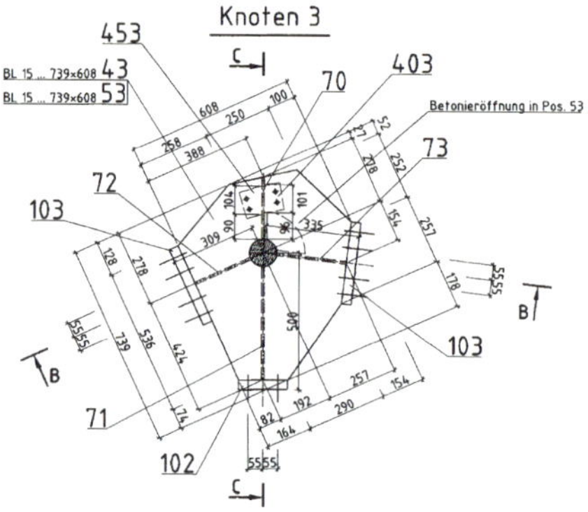

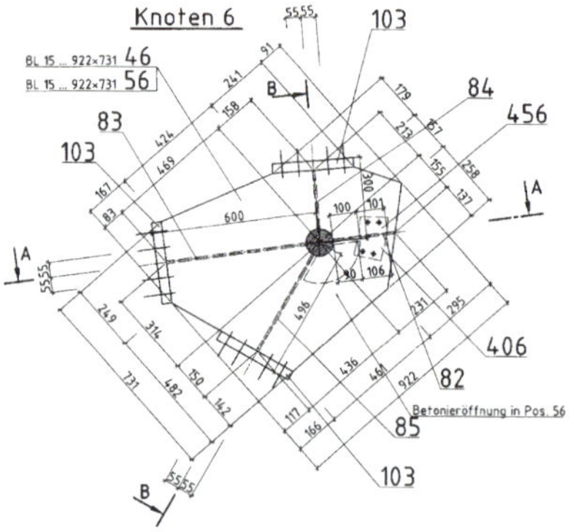

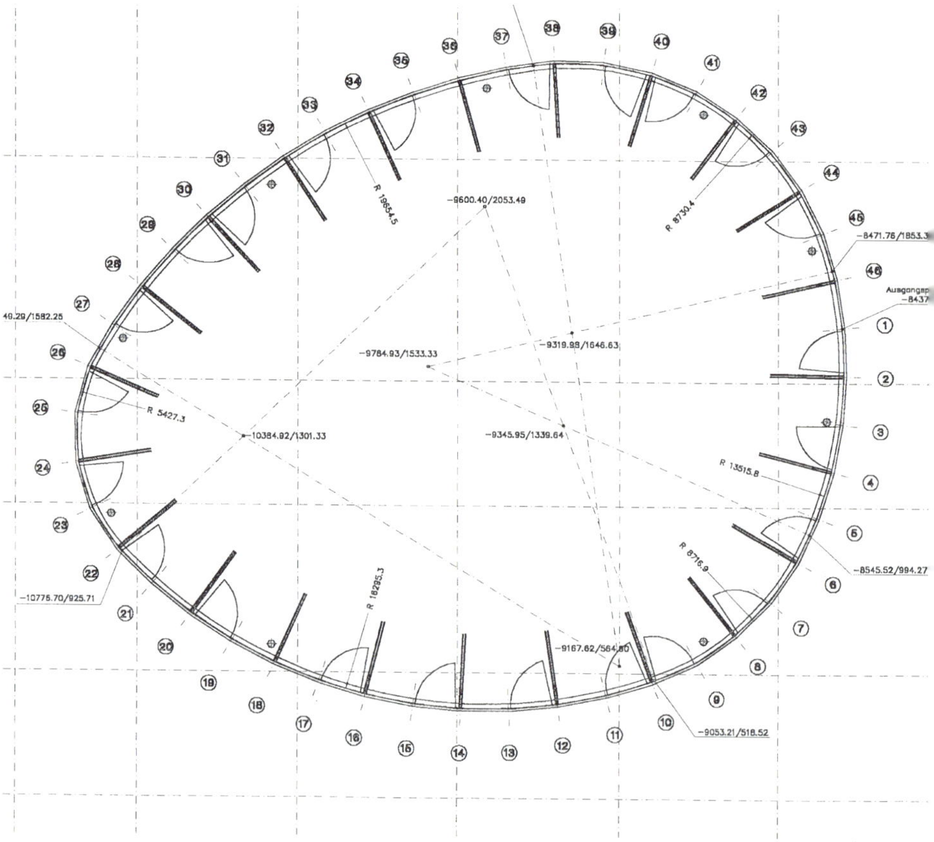
R 19654.5
-9600.40/2053.49
R 8730.4
49.29/1582.25
-9319.99/1646.63
-9784.93/1533.33
R 5427.3
-10384.92/1301.33
-9345.95/1339.64
R 13515.8
R 8716.9
-8545.52/994.27
-10776.70/925.71
R 18295.3
-9167.62/564.60
-9053.21/518.52

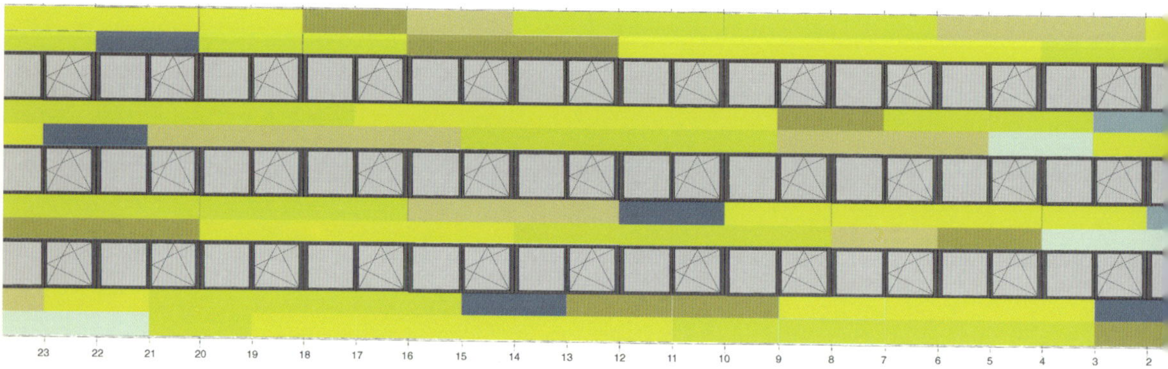
23 22 21 20 19 18 17 16 15 14 13 12 11 10 9 8 7 6 5 4 3 2

Fassadenabwicklung Pillbox (Wellblechverkleidung)
Elevation pillbox cladding (corrugated metal panels)

Betonfertigteile der Brüstung
Precast concrete upstands

Auskragung nach Süden
Cantilever towards the south

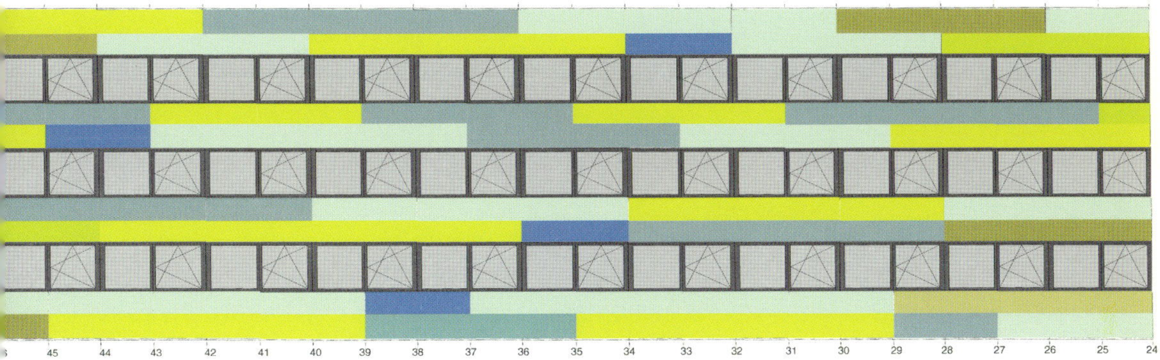

Altbau

Der Altbau gehörte ursprünglich zu dem von den Architekten Schwebes, Schoszberger und Noth in den 50er-Jahren entworfenen Ensemble des Graphischen und Gewerbezentrums (GGZ). Seit 1961 im Besitz der GSW wurde der elegante Sichtbetonbau in den 70er-Jahren entsprechend der neuen Wärmeschutzverordnung mit einer Wärmedämmung versehen.
Die damals aufgebrachte Fassadenverkleidung aus Faserzementplatten wurde jetzt entfernt und sachgerecht entsorgt. Eine neue Verkleidung des (inzwischen asbestfreien) gleichen Produkts wurde wieder aufgebracht. Die ebenfalls damals eingebauten Doppelfenster und Sonnenschutzeinrichtungen wurden erhalten.
Im Innern des Gebäudes wurden alle Trennwände, Decken und Fussböden erneuert sowie die Beleuchtung und Verkabelung dem neuesten Stand angepasst. Ein (jetzt überflüssig gewordenes) Treppenhaus wurde entfernt und durch Büroflächen ersetzt.

Existing Tower

The existing tower was originally part of the ensemble of the *Graphisches und Gewerbezentrum* (GGZ) designed by the architects Schwebes Schoszberger und Noth in the 1950s. Occupied by GSW since 1961, the elegant concrete building was completely reclad in the '70s in compliance with new legislation on energy saving.
In the current refurbishment the cladding from the '70s was removed and disposed of. Replacement asbestos-free boards (from the original company) were mounted. The windows and louvre blinds which had been installed as part of the '70s renovation were retained.
Internally all partition walls, ceilings and flooring were renewed, and lighting and data networks were replaced. A staircase which had become superfluous was removed to create additional office space.

BUS
Coca-Cola

Detail der Fassadenzementplatten-Verkleidung mit unsichtbarer Verankerung. Die Stützenverkleidung wurde an den Schmalseiten als durchgängiges U-Profil ausgeführt, im Erdgeschossbereich ist die Ecke mit einer integrierten Edelstahlschiene verstärkt.
Cladding detail of the fibre-cement panels with invisible fixing. The smaller ends of the column cladding were made as continuous U-profiles; on the ground floor the corners are reinforced with stainless steel.

Baugrube
Excavation

Grundriss eines Obergeschosses Altbau und Neubau
mit zweihüftiger Büroaufteilung

Plan of the existing tower the new double-banked office floor

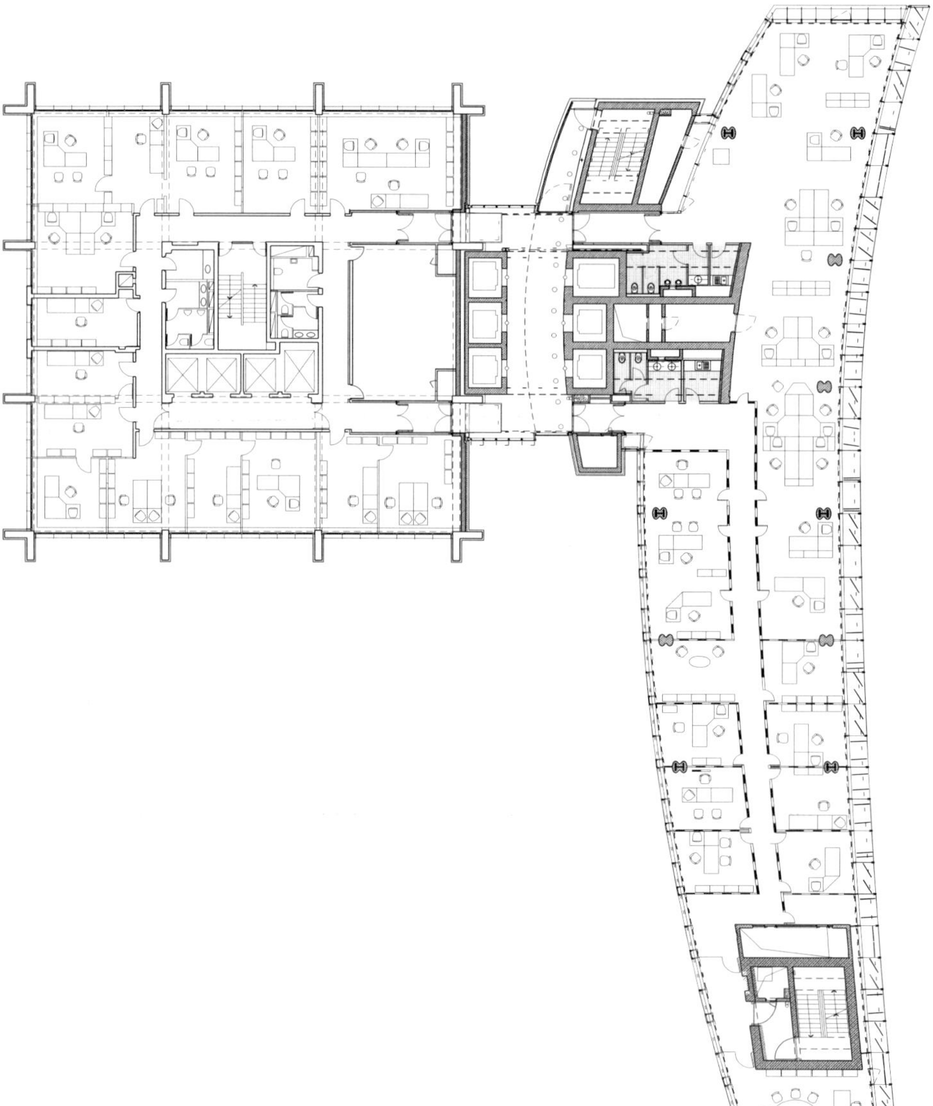

Hochhaus

Das Hochhaus ist der Gebäudeteil, der sich (in der beinahe didaktischen Entwicklung einzelner Volumen aus der Interpretation verschiedener Stadtideen) am stärksten an der Gegenwart und Zukunft orientiert. Städtebaulich reagiert die Scheibe in erster Linie auf den Altbau und den Kontext der 50er- und 60er-Jahre, in seiner Gebäudephilosophie versucht sie, die Zukunft zu antizipieren.
Das Niedrigenergiekonzept des Gebäudes bezieht sich im Wesentlichen auf diesen Bauteil, sein ästhetischer Anspruch verlässt den Rahmen des Dagewesenen. Das Hochhaus gibt dem Gebäudekomplex seine weitreichende städtebauliche Präsenz und Aura.

High-rise

The high-rise slab is the building element which – in the almost didactic reference of the individual volumes to corresponding urban ideas from different generations – is mostly associated with the present and the future. In urban terms it reacts to the surrounding buildings of the '50s and '60s, with its architectural philosophy it attempts to anticipate the future. The project's low-energy concepts are embodied in the high-rise, whose aesthetic goes beyond the limits of the known. It is the high-rise which lends the whole ensemble its urbane presence and aura.

AXEL SPRINGER VERLAG
BERLINISCHE LEBEN

230 82 80

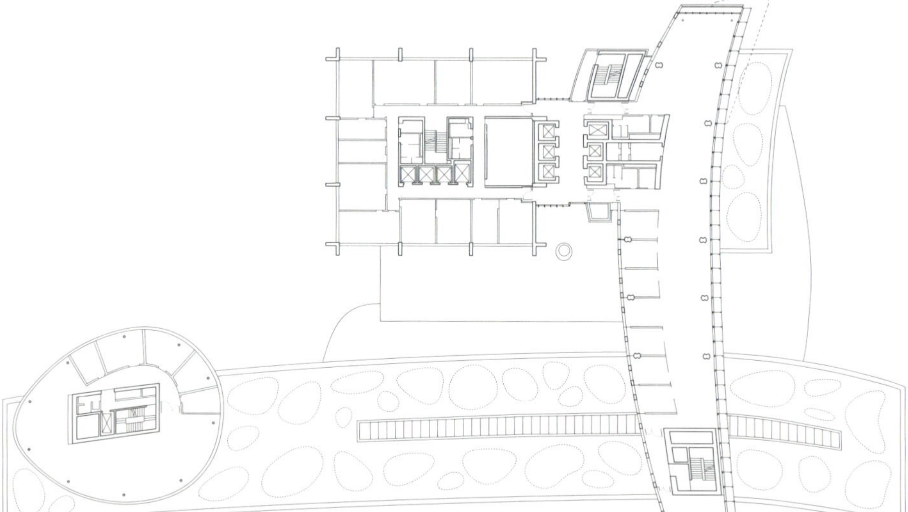

Modell M. 1:150 von Norden
Model scale 1:150 from the north

Grundriss 3. Obergeschoss M. ca. 1:1000
Third floor plan scale ca. 1:1000

Schnitt Eingangshalle und Tiefgarage M. ca. 1:1000
Section of the entrance hall and parking garage scale ca. 1:1000

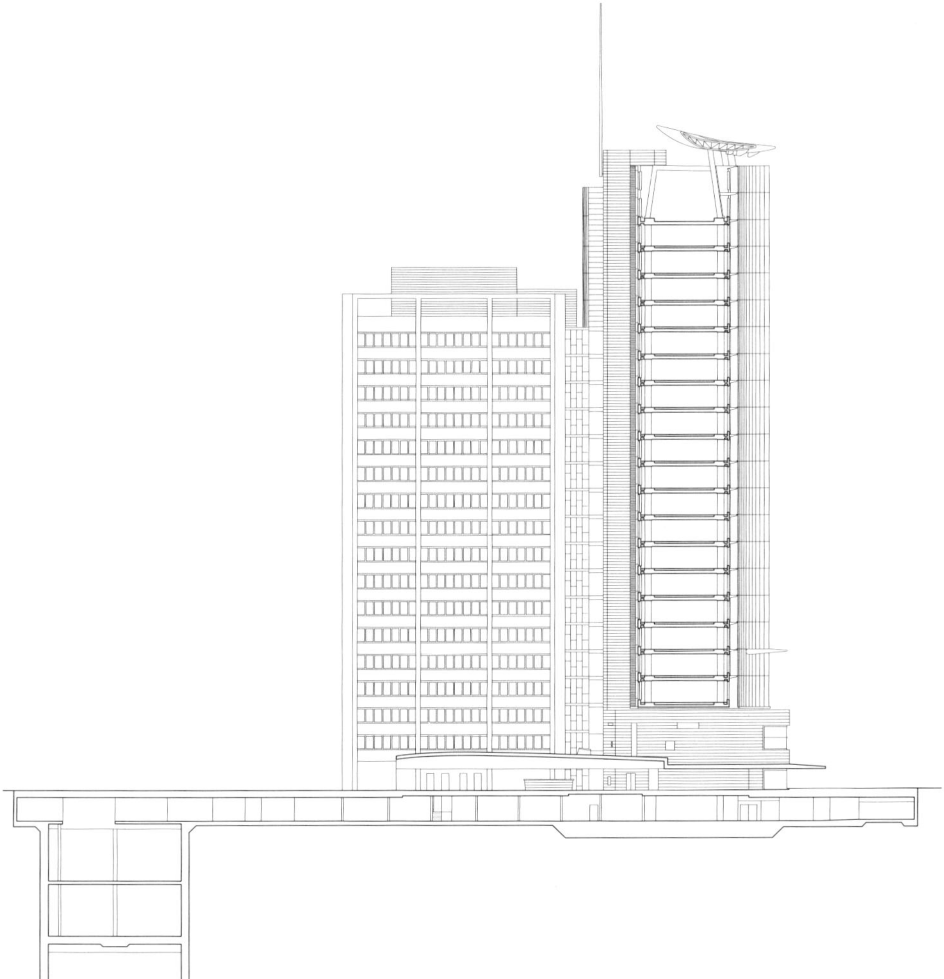

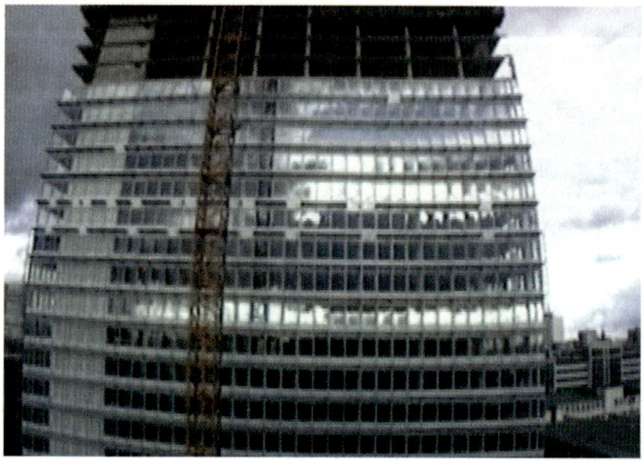

Rohbaukonstruktion

Die Struktur des Hochhauses erfuhr nach dem Wettbewerb eine entscheidende Änderung: Was ursprünglich als einhüftiges Konstruktionsprinzip gedacht war, sollte nach der Meinung einschlägiger Gutachter einen zweihüftigen Grundriss aufnehmen. Auf Grund dieser Änderung in den Anforderungen an das Gebäude, musste die Konstruktion der Hochhausscheibe neu gedacht werden. Insbesondere die Auskragung an beiden Enden und die Überbrückung der Eingangshalle (die bislang mit einer statischen Rückgratwand überbrückt werden sollte) musste jetzt anders bewältigt werden.
Zur Ausführung kam deshalb eine vom Rohbauunternehmer vorgeschlagene Konstruktion, die die Lasten über zwei längsverlaufende Spannbetonunterzüge geschossweise abträgt. Zwischen diesen Längsträgern spannen Betonplatten, die, halbvorgefertigt geliefert, auf der Baustelle mit Aufbeton versehen wurden; so wurde für die Unterdecken eine Betonoberfläche mit Ausbaustandard erreicht. Denn das, was sich normalerweise hinter abgehängten Decken verbirgt, ist hier in die Rohdecke integriert. Eine Reihe von Querschlitzen und ein Längsschlitz am Deckenrand enthalten Belichtung, Sprinkler- und Brandmeldeanlage.
Die Stützenform des Hauses ist aus dem Formprofil eines Doppel-T-Trägers und der aus Brandschutzgründen erforderlichen Betonüberdeckung entstanden. Mit dieser ökonomischen Lösung wurden Material und Raum gespart und ein sehr eleganter Stützenkörper geschaffen.

Structure

The structure of the high-rise building was changed after the competition. The originally asymetrical design had to be adapted to suit a double-banked office plan (following the advice of a number of consultant institutes).

In particular the cantilevers at each end of the building and the bridging across the entrance hall (which until now had been achieved by the so-called *spine wall*) had now to be resolved differently.

In the final concept (which was suggested by the contractors) the cantilevers are carried on every floor by a post-stressed RC edge beam between which span prefabricated floor elements with an in-situ concrete topping.

As these smooth concrete ceilings remain exposed (as part of the low-energy concept) everything which is normally concealed behind a suspended ceiling is integrated into the primary structure. An even rhythm of slots in the ceiling contains lighting, sprinklers and smoke-alarms (with a recess along the façades enabling the lateral connections).

The columns of the building have a special form. They were developed from the section of a steel I-beam and its concrete fire protection. The resulting outline is the most economical solution in terms of space and material and provides a very elegant form.

ZÜBLIN

Konstruktion der endgültigen Hochhausdecke nach einem Sondervorschlag des Rohbauunternehmers

Final high-rise floor construction after a proposal from the contractors regarding the edge beam

Grundriss Hochhaus 18. Obergeschoss M. ca. 1:400

Plan of the high-rise 18th floor scale ca. 1:400

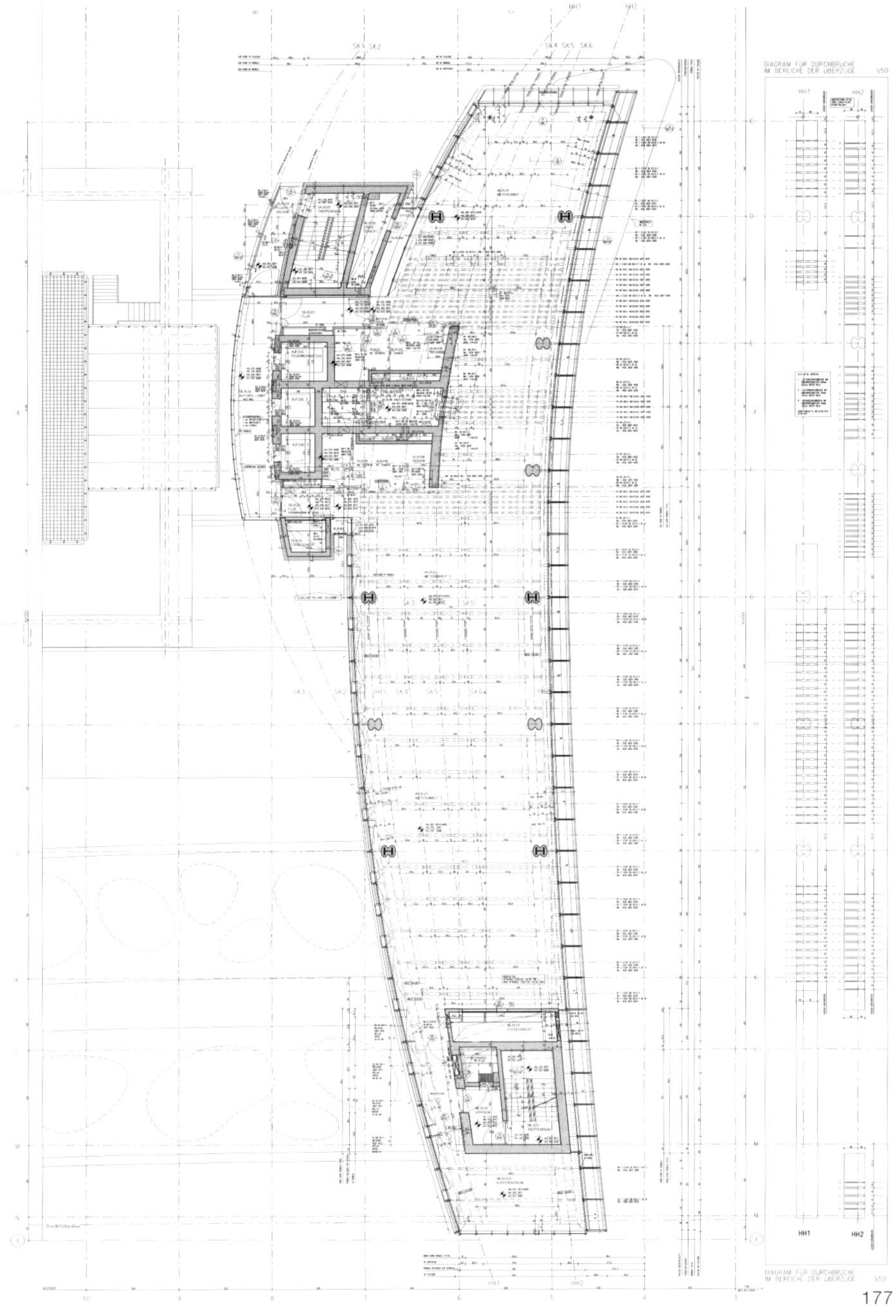

Querschnitt Deckenrandträger mit schlaffer und Spannkabel-Bewehrung
Cross section of the edge beam with stressed and non-stressed reinforcement

Detail Längsschnitt und Grundriss Deckenrandträger mit Spannkabelführung
Partial long section and plan of the edge beam with tension cables

Armierungseisen und Spannkabel, Balkenkopf
Reinforcement cages and tension cables within the edge beam

Auskragende Rohbaukonstruktion Nordseite
Cantilevering structure on the north side

Überbrückung Eingangshalle
Structure bridging the entrance hall

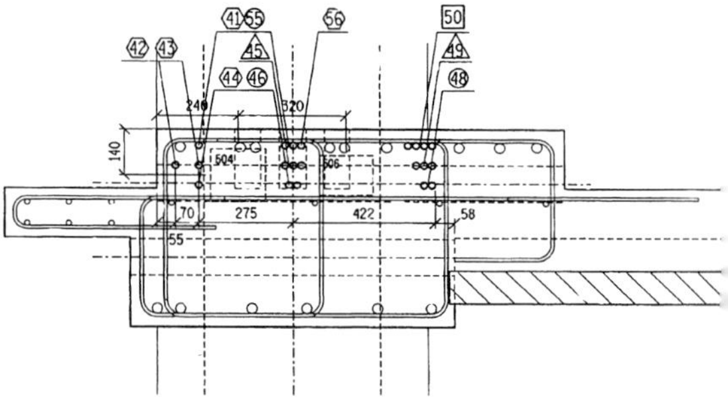

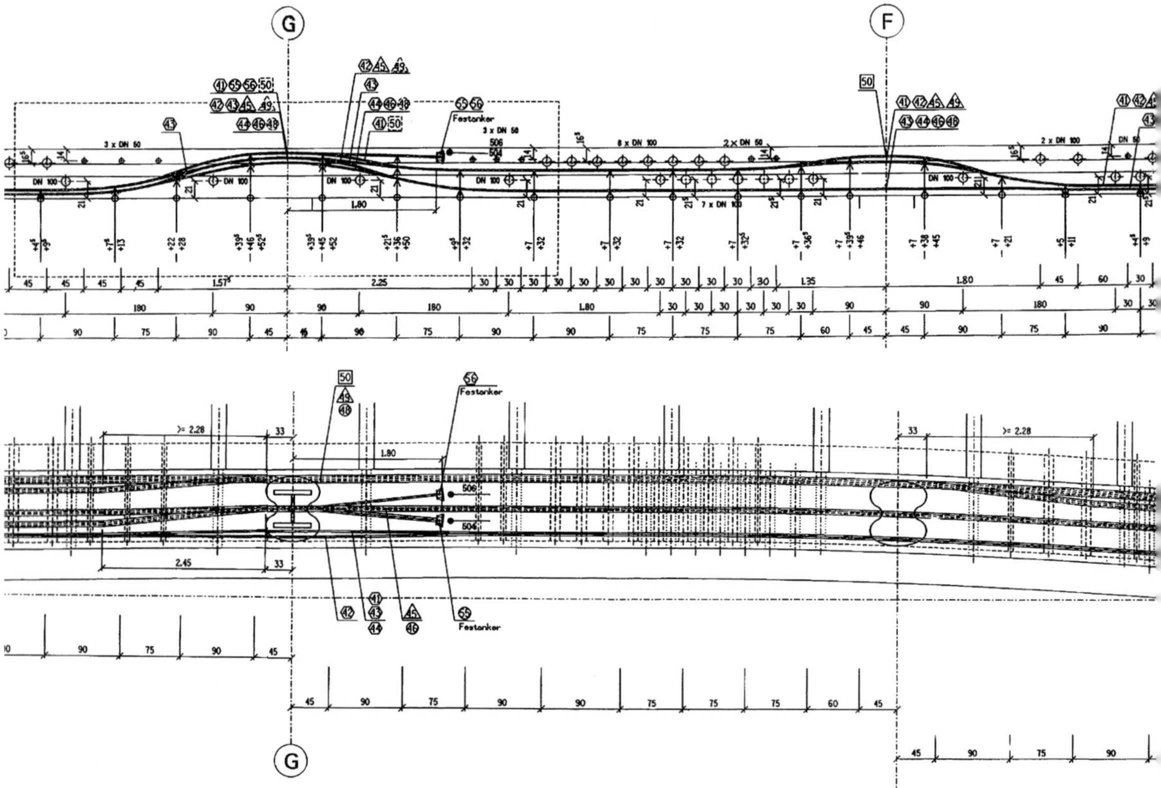

Grundriss Stahlverbundstütze
Plan of concrete composite column

Schalung für Randträger und Stütze
Shuttering for edge beam and column

Rohbauskelett Hochhaus
Structural carcass of the high-rise building

Stahlschalung für die Stützen
Steel formwork for the columns

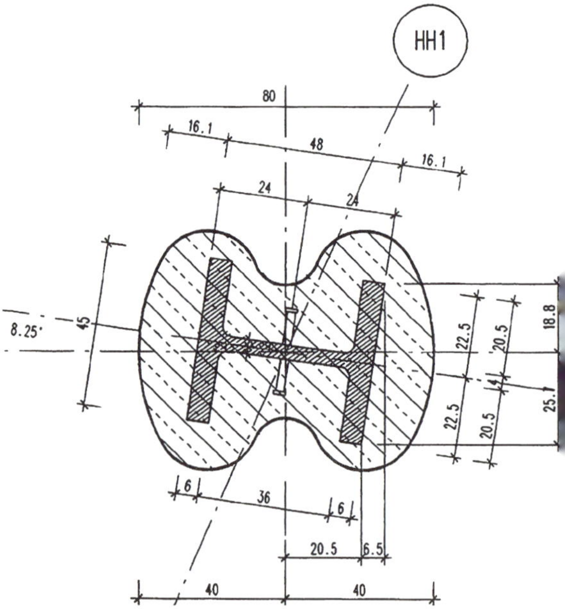

Niedrigenergiekonzept

Die ersten Wettbewerbsvorschläge für Gebäudetechnik wurden im Laufe der Planung in ein Niedrigenergiekonzept mit sechs Punkten umgesetzt. Um dieses weitgehend passive (low-tech) Konzept zu verfeinern, bedienten sich Architekten und Ingenieure bei der Planung diverser (high-tech) computergenerierter Simulationsprogramme. Darüber hinaus wurde das Gebäude zweimal im Windkanal des *Department of Aerospace Engineering* in Bristol analysiert.
Mit Hilfe der Ergebnisse dieser Analysen soll Heizungs-, Lüftungs- und Beleuchtungsenergie in wesentlichem Umfang eingespart werden und die Aufenthaltsqualität im Gebäude mit natürlichen Mitteln soweit optimiert werden, dass ein Standard erreicht wird, der mit einem technischen Lüftungs-, Beleuchtungs- und Klimatisierungskonzept vergleichbar ist.

Low-energy Concept

The first ideas of the competition scheme have been developed into a low-energy concept of six points. In this the design team employed (high-tech) computer-generated simulation programmes to materialize a mostly passive (low-tech) concept. The building was analysed twice in the wind-tunnel of the Department of Aerospace Engineering in Bristol.
Founded on the results of these analyses, the aim is a significant reduction in energy input for heating, ventilation and lighting. The environmental qualities achieved in the building with natural means are to match those normally created with technical ventilation and air conditioning systems.

Sparkasse

Das Gebäude wurde während der Planung in mehreren CFD (Computational Fluid Dynamics)-Analysen der Ingenieure in seinem thermischen und Lüftungsverhalten untersucht. Hier wurden nicht nur Luftströme berechnet, um Öffnungsquerschnitte zu bestimmen, und Temperaturentwicklungen vorherbestimmt, um den Einsatz von Sonnenschutz und Speichermasse auszuloten, sondern es wurde auch das Funktionieren der Konvektionsfassade selbst simuliert. Mit Hilfe dieser komplexen Programme gelang es ausserdem, ein schlüssiges Brandschutzkonzept zu erarbeiten. Die Anwendung der an sich einfachen, aber schwer zu definierenden Prinzipien der Querlüftung konnte so mit an Sicherheit grenzender Wahrscheinlichkeit geplant werden.

The engineers investigated the thermal and ventilation performance of the building using CFD (computational fluid dynamics) analyses. These programmes established the air flows so that the ventilation openings could be dimensioned, and predicted the range of room temperatures so that, taking the thermal mass into account, the solar shading could be designed. In addition, the way in which the solar flue would function could be simulated. With the help of these complex programmes it was possible to devise a consistent concept for fire protection. Thus, the application of CFD analyses enabled the engineers to predict with a high degree of certainty the way in which the seemingly simple, yet otherwise unpredictable principles of cross ventilation would work.

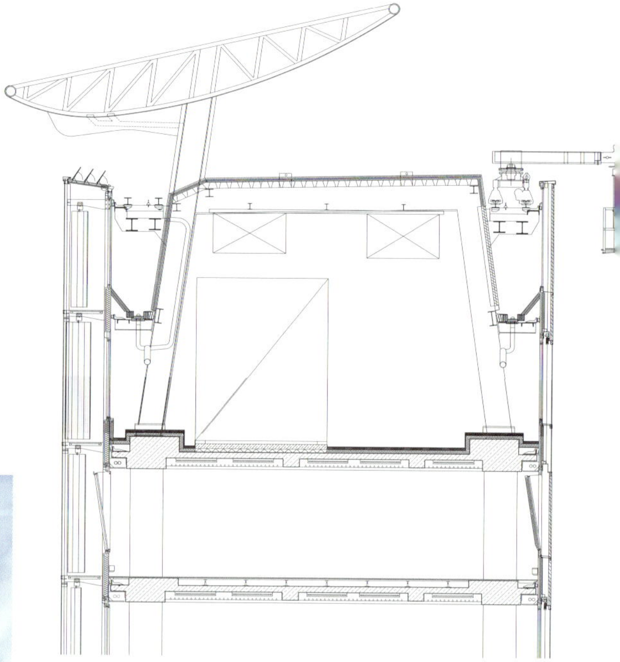

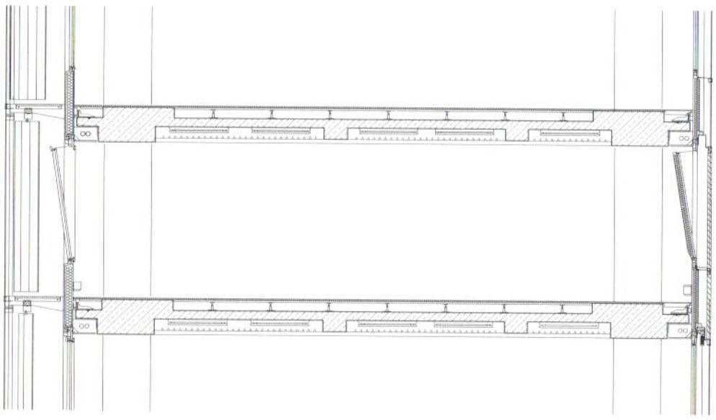

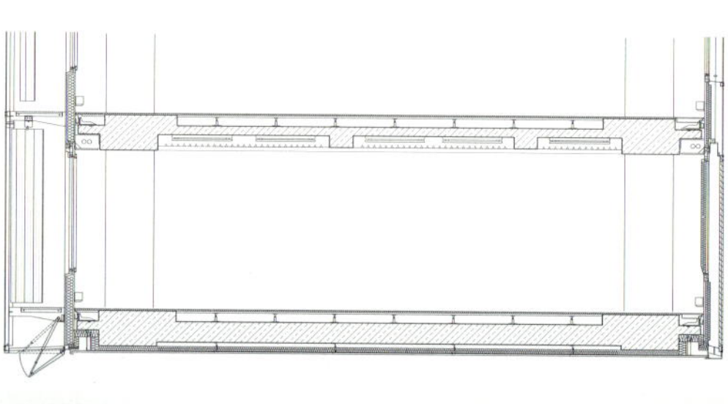

Prinzipschnitt Hochhaus
Principle high-rise section

Ausschnitt aus CFD-Analyse
Image from CFD analysis

Blick in den Zwischenraum der Konvektionsfassade
View into the space of the solar flue

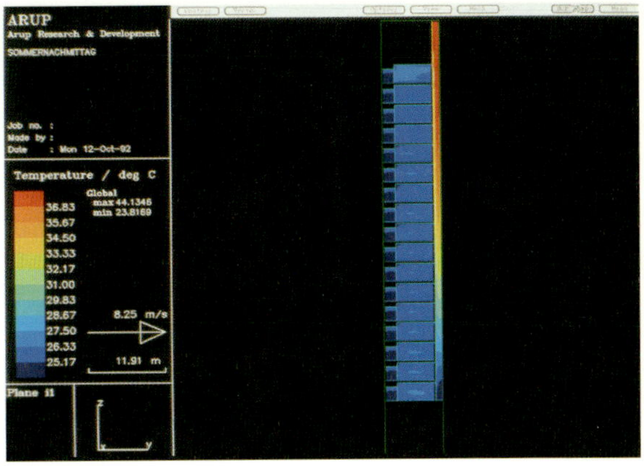

CFD-Analyse: Temperaturen im Hochhaus
CFD analysis: temperatures in the high-rise

Sommermorgen
summer morning

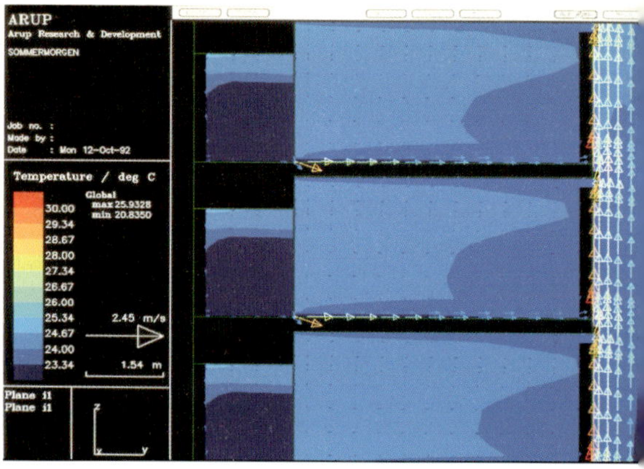

Sommernachmittag
summer afternoon

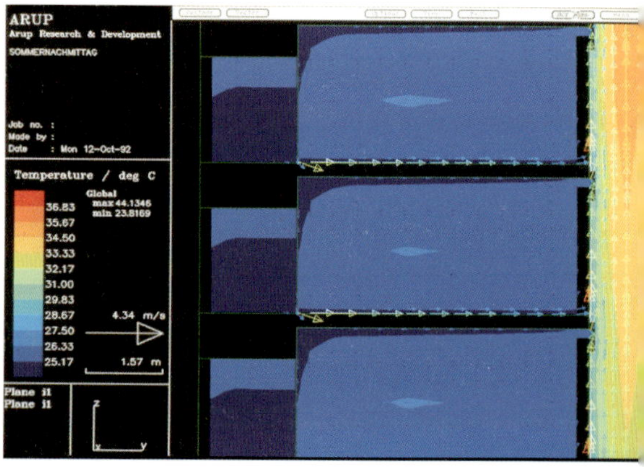

Sommernacht
summer night

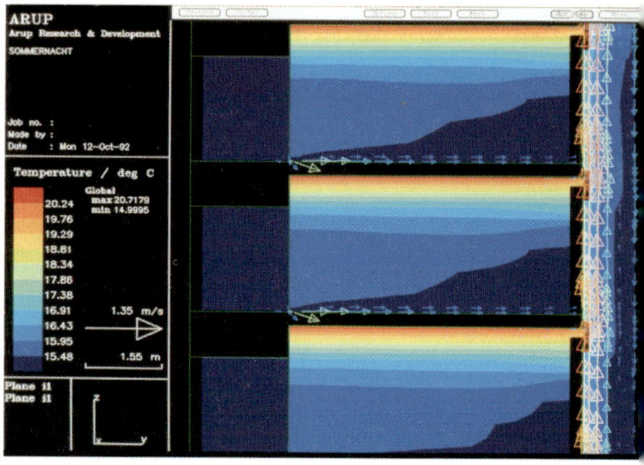

Wintertag
winter day

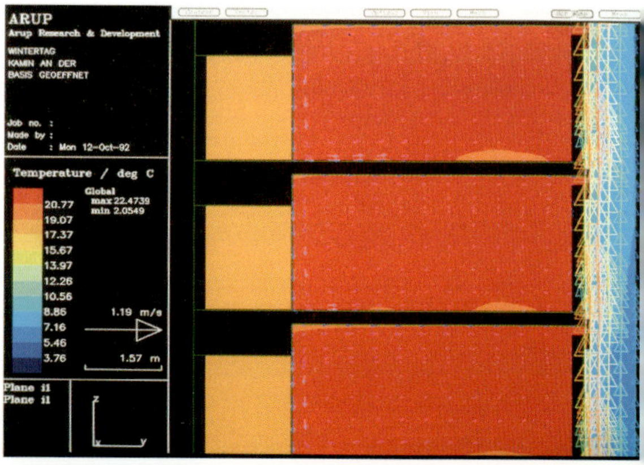

Verhalten des Abzugschachtes im Brandfall
Performance of the solar flue in case of fire

nach 60 Sekunden
after 60 seconds

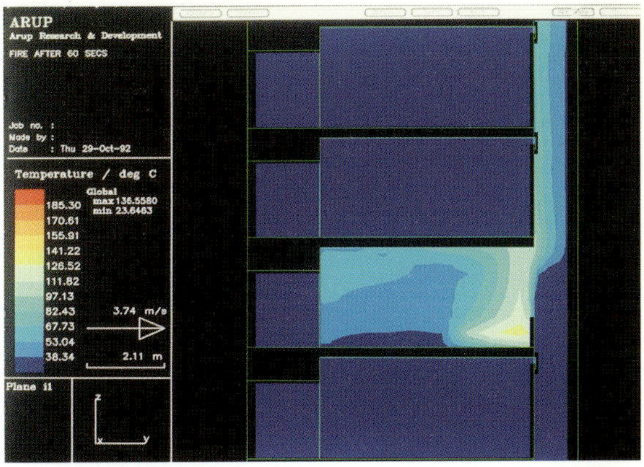

nach 120 Sekunden
after 120 seconds

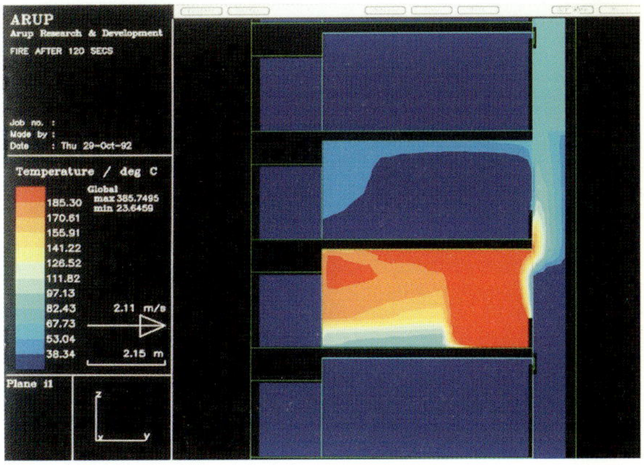

nach 200 Sekunden
after 200 seconds

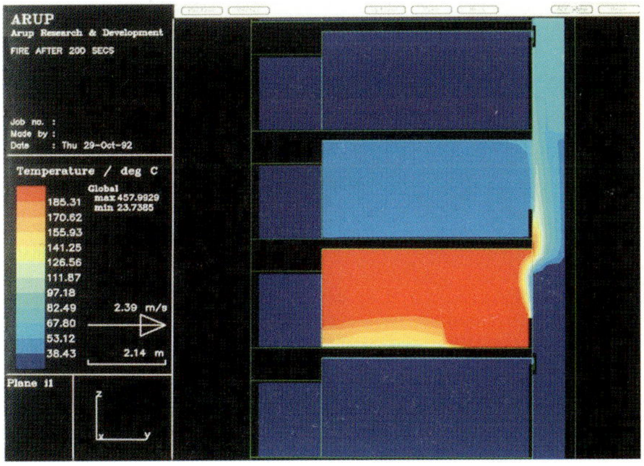

nach 300 Sekunden
after 300 seconds

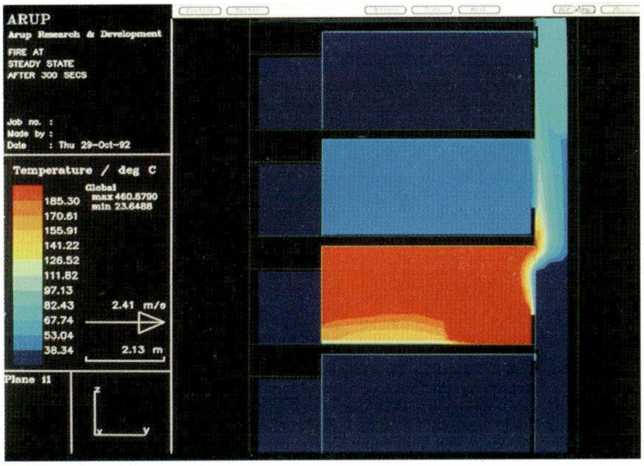

Betrieb tagsüber

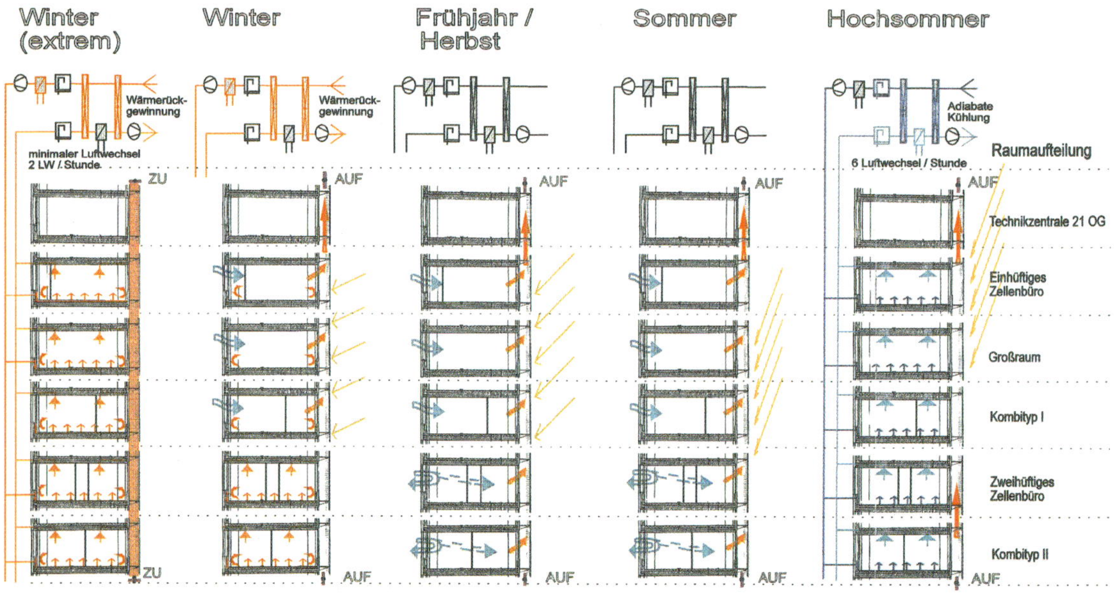

Außentemperaturen :

unter 5°

Mechanische Belüftung
Thermische Fassade als Puffer
Statische Heizung an
Luftklappen oben und unten zu

5° bis 15 °

Natürliche Querlüftung ab 5 Grad.
etwa 2 Luftwechsel / Stunde
Statische Heizung an.
Mieter können mechanische Belüftung einschalten, wenn sie wollen.

15° bis 20°

Natürliche Querlüftung von 15 bis 20 Grad.
zwischen 2 und 6 Luftwechsel / Stunde
Statische Heizung aus.
Mieter können mechanische Belüftung einschalten, wenn sie wollen.

20° bis 25°

Natürliche Querlüftung bis 25 Grad.
etwa 6 Luftwechsel / Stunde
Statische Heizung aus.
Mieter können mechanische Belüftung einschalten, wenn sie wollen.

über 25°

Adiabate Kühlung und
6 Lüftwechsel / Stunde
mechanische Lüftung
Thermische Fassade führt Wärme ab und beschattet das Gebäude

Legende :

- Zuluft
- Abluft
- Heizung
- mechanische Zuluft, gekühlt
- mechanische Abluft
- mechanische Zuluft, warm
- mechanische Abluft

Betrieb nachts

Winter (extr.) | Winter | Frühjahr/ Herbst | Sommer | Hochsommer

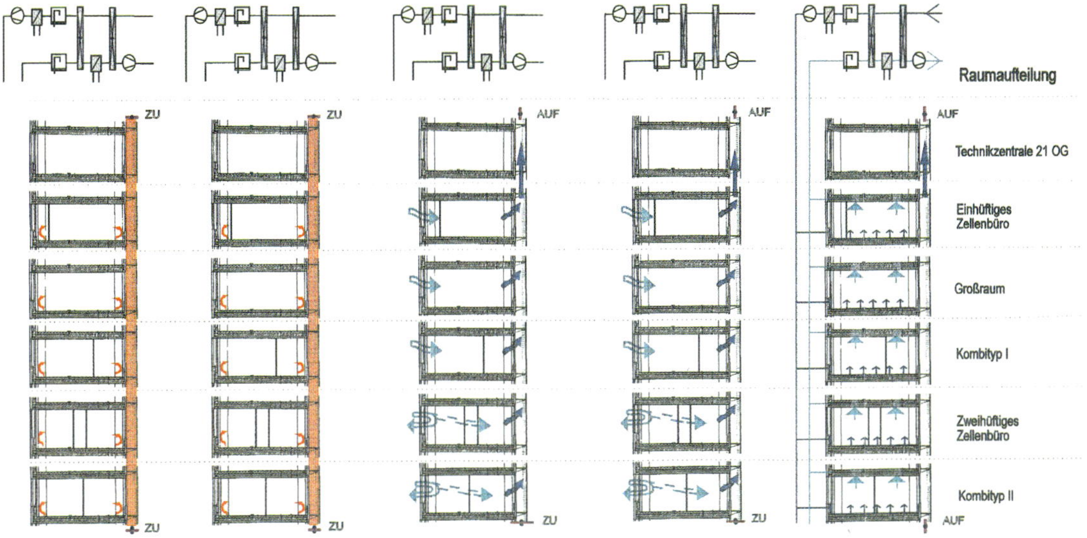

Winter (extr.)
Außentemperaturen (nachts)
unter 5°
Statische Heizung an
Doppelfassade als Wärmepuffer
Klappen geschlossen

Winter
unter 5°
Statische Heizung an
Doppelfassade als Wärmepuffer
Klappen geschlossen

Frühjahr/Herbst
5° bis 10°
Thermischer Auftrieb durch Kamineffekt
Natürliche Nachtkühlung und Belüftung
Klappe unten geschlossen

Sommer
10° bis 15°
Thermischer Auftrieb
durch Kamineffekt
Natürliche Vorkühlung in der Nacht
Klappe unten geschlossen

Hochsommer
über 15°
Mechanische Belüftung
in der Nacht
kühlt das Gebäude vor
Klappen geöffnet

Legende :
- Zuluft
- Abluft
- Heizung
- mechanische Zuluft
- mechanische Abluft

Natürliche Querlüftung

Der in der Konvektionsfassade durch natürlichen Wärmeauftrieb entstehende Unterdruck wird benutzt, um frische Luft durch das Gebäude hindurchzuziehen. Wenn Fenster auf der Ost- bzw. der Westseite des Gebäudes geöffnet werden, fliesst frische Luft von Ost nach West durch das Gebäude. Diese Luftbewegung ist auf Grund der durch Klappen regelbaren, gleichmässigen Druckverhältnisse in der Doppelfassade von Aussenbedingungen weitgehend unabhängig und garantiert damit Luftwechselraten, die mit mechanischen Lüftungen vergleichbar sind.

Natural cross ventilation

The convection in the western double façade creates a negative pressure which can pull fresh air through the building. When windows on the two façades are opened, fresh air flows from east to west. Due to control flaps at the top and bottom of the solar flue this air flow is more or less independent from outside conditions and enables air exchange rates which are comparable to mechanical systems.

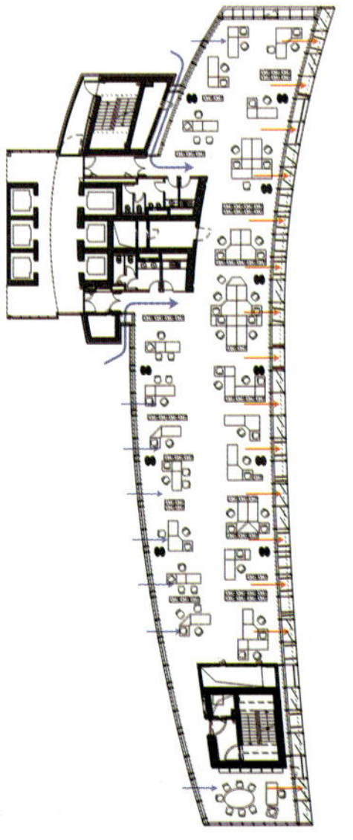

großraum ***open plan***

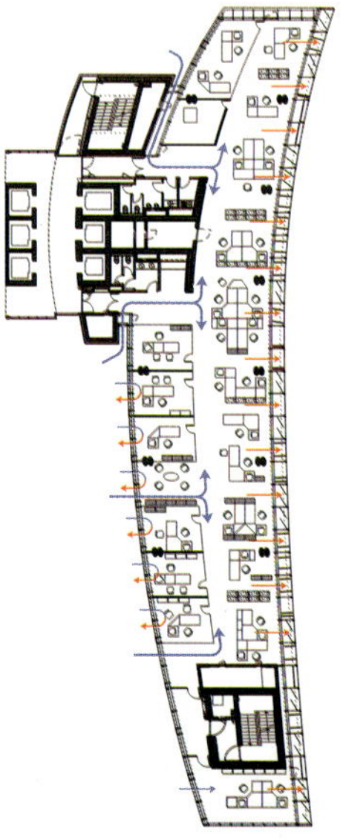

kombi/ost ***combi/east***

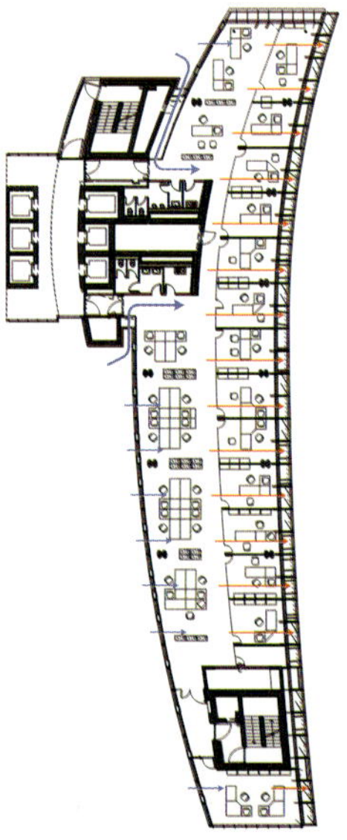

kombi/west ***combi/west***

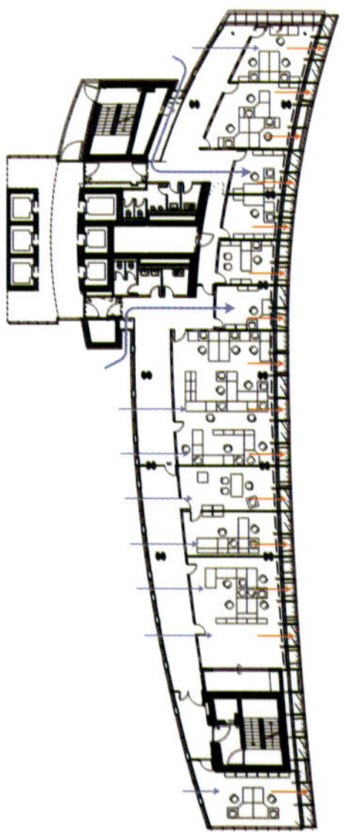

einhüftig *single banked*

Luftzirkulation bei verschiedenen Grundrissvarianten

Air flow in different plan layouts

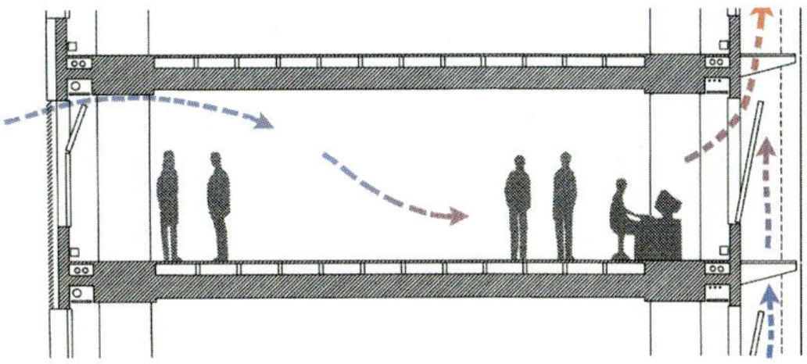

querlüftung - großraum *cross ventilation - open plan*

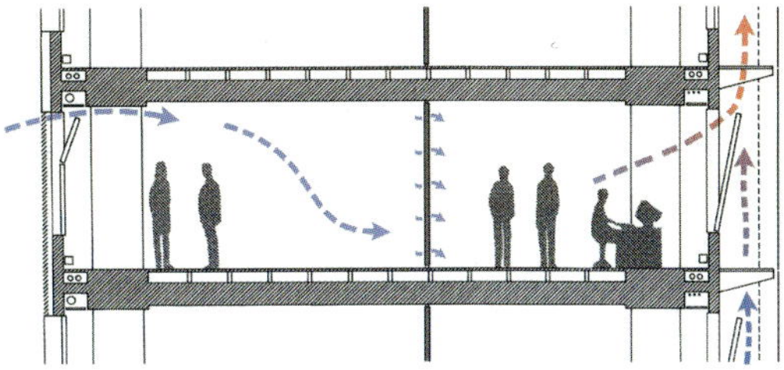

querlüftung - kombi/ost *cross ventilation - combi/east*

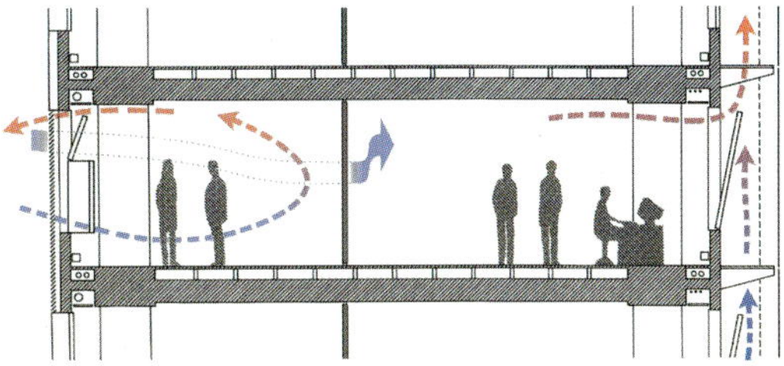

querlüftung - kombi/west *cross ventilation - combi/west*

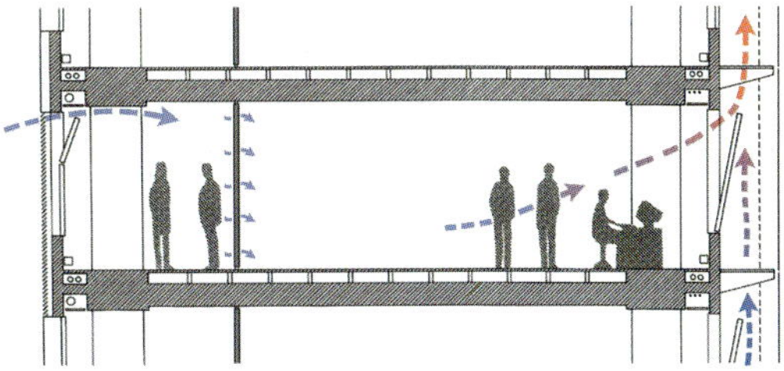

querlüftung - einhüftig cross ventilation - single banked

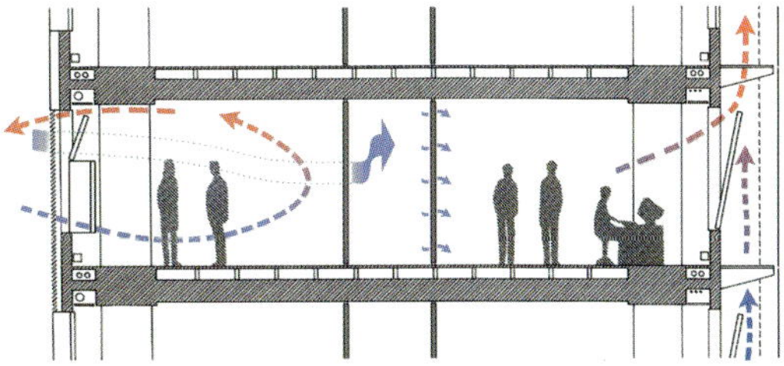

querlüftung - zweihüftig *cross ventilation - double banked*

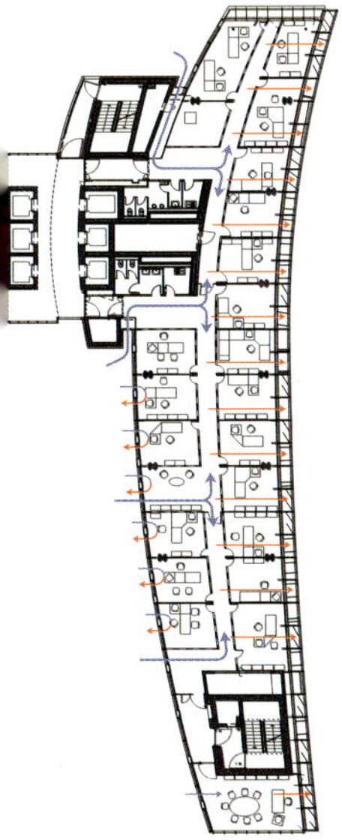

zweihüftig *double banked*

Westfassade unteres Abschlussdetail

Air intake detail on the under side of the solar flue

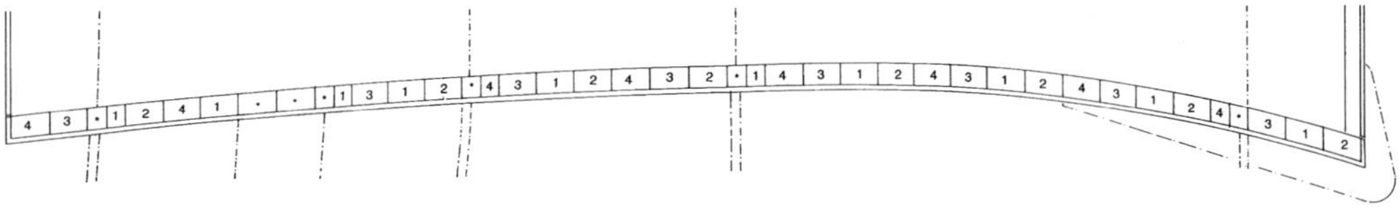

öffnungsdiagramm 1/200

betr. öffnungsdiagramm oben

alle klappen 1	12,5%	der gesammtfassade offen
alle klappen 1,2	25%	der gesammtfassade offen
alle klappen 1,2,3	37,5%	der gesammtfassade offen
alle klappen 1,2,3,4	50%	der gesammtfassade offen

* nicht zu öffnen klappflügel

siehe auch entwurfsbericht von Arup feb (95) Rev A,
und arup zeichnung M 60 04 Ind B

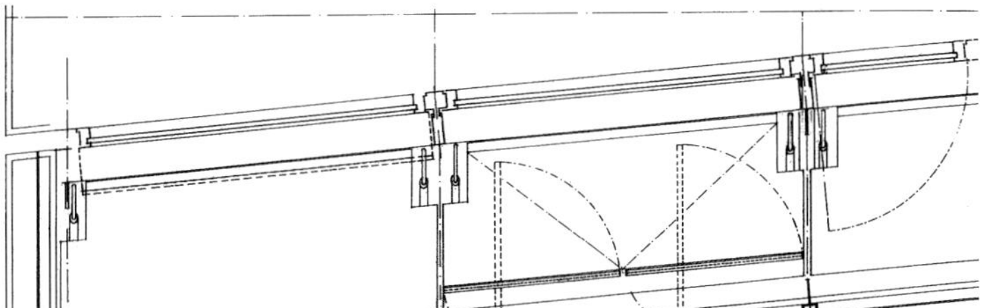

grundriss 1/20

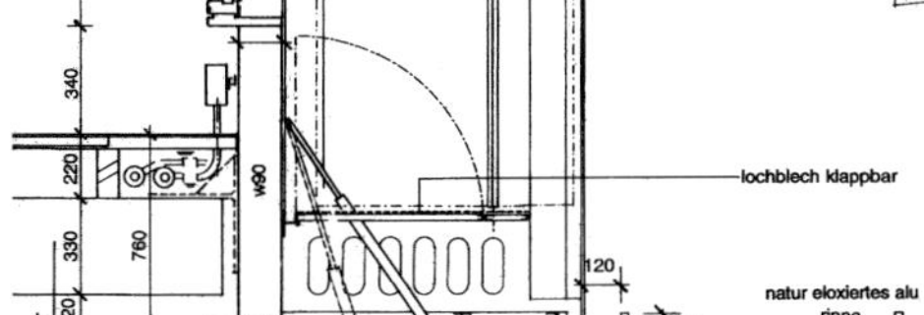

querschnitt 1/20

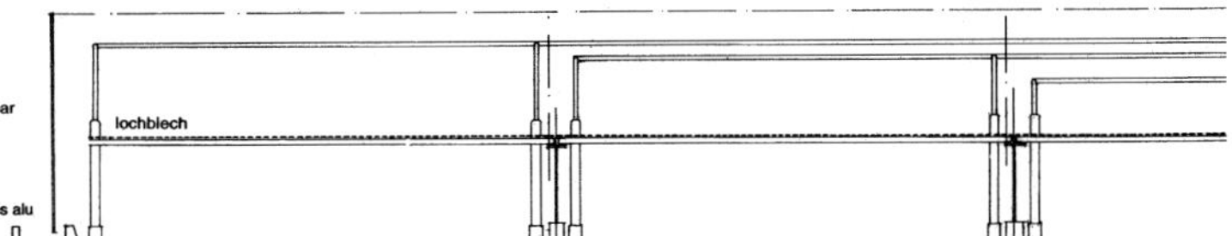

längsschnitt 1/20

Überstromelement

Das Überstromelement wurde speziell entwickelt, um die natürliche Lüftung des Gebäudes auch über geschlossene bzw. verglaste Längswände hinweg zu ermöglichen. Als Bestandteil der Tür hat es geringere Brandschutzanforderungen als die Wand, durch seine schallabsorbierende Füllung erreicht es einen Schalldämmwert, der dem der Tür entspricht.

Ventilation panel

This ventilation panel was developed to enable cross ventilation through walls – whether glazed or solid – which run parallel to the long façades. Designed as a part of the door, it has to fulfil only reduced fire protection requirements. With its sound absorbent lining, the panel achieves a sound insulation value similar to that of the door.

Horizontalschnitt Tür und Überstromelement (Entwurf)

Horizontal section through corridor door and ventilation panel (design stage)

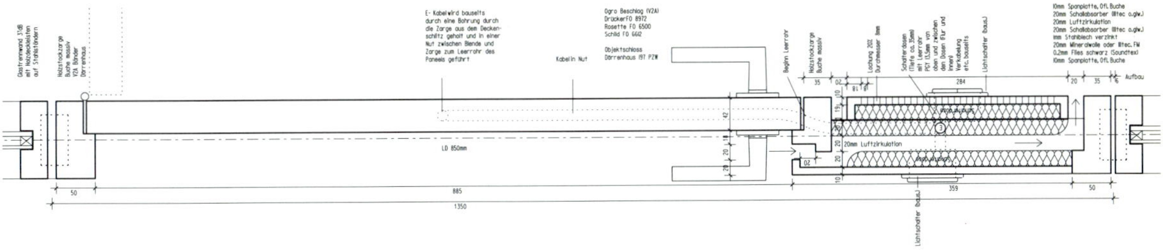

Optimierung der Tagesbelichtung

Durch eine sehr grosszügige Verglasung der gesamten Fassade wird die Tagesbelichtung der Büroflächen optimiert. Der Grundriss des Gebäudes ist relativ schmal, sodass die natürliche Belichtung der Arbeitsplätze während der Arbeitszeiten fast über das ganze Jahr gewährleistet ist.

Ausbildung von Pufferzonen

Um eine Minimierung des Transmissions-Wärmeverlustes der Fassaden zu erreichen, sind sowohl die östliche als auch die westliche Aussenwand mit Pufferzonen in Form von zweischichtigen Fassaden ausgestattet. Die Ostfassade verfügt über eine ca. 20 cm tiefe, geschossweise hinterlüftete Doppelhaut. Auf der Westseite ist der Zwischenraum zwischen der isolierverglasten Innenseite und der einfachverglasten Aussenseite 1 m tief. Die Westseite ist als Konvektionsfassade ausgebildet, die die gesamte Fläche der Fassade abdeckt.

Maximum daylight

Generous window-sizes create optimum daylight conditions on the office floors. As the plan of the building is relatively narrow all workplaces are daylit during office hours for most of the year.

Buffer zones

To minimize heat loss both the east- and the west-perimeter-walls are designed to be double façades. The east-façade, with two glass skins spaced 20 cm apart, is ventilated on every floor. On the west-side the space between glass layers is 1 m deep, and continuous allowing this face to act as a solar flue.

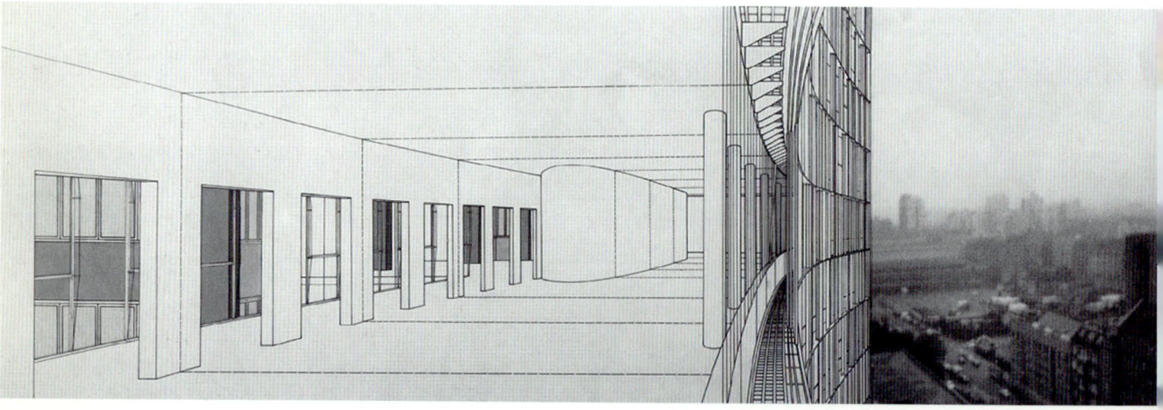

Innenperspektive Hochhausgeschoss
Interior perspective of high-rise shell

Ausschnitt Grundriss Westfassade
Detail plan west façade

Bemusterung Sonnenschutzläden bei der Fassadenfirma
Inspection of solar shutter mock-ups at the manufacturer's

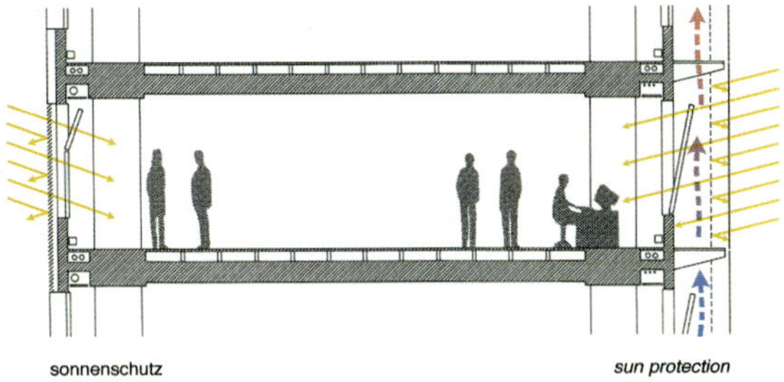

Effektiver Sonnenschutz

Zwischen den Schichten der zweischaligen Ost- und Westfassade sind individuell bewegliche Sonnenschutzelemente angeordnet, die die Sonnenstrahlung vom Innenraum fernhalten. Diese Elemente werden wie die Fensteröffnungen der Fassade von jedem Nutzer individuell, aber auch zentral gesteuert, sodass im Sommer z.B. die morgendliche Aufheizung der Büroräume effektiv vermieden werden kann.

Solar protection

The building interior is protected from solar radiation through flexible blinds placed between the glass layers of the two façades. These elements – like the windows – are controlled by the individual occupant; but a central building management system also activates them twice dayly in order to avoid overheating in the morning or afternoon respectively.

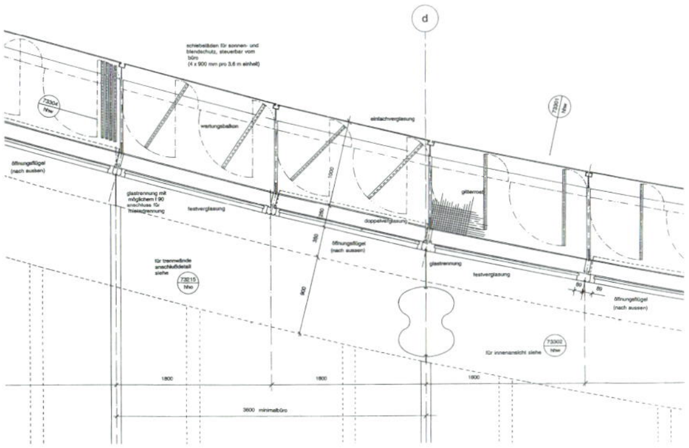

Ausnutzung der Speichermassen

Die Decken des Gebäudes wurden generell ohne Verkleidung ausgeführt, um die thermische Masse des Stahlbetontragwerks zur positiven Beeinflussung des Raumklimas einzusetzen. Insbesondere im Sommer wird die thermische Trägheit des massiven Materials genutzt, um das Gebäude, das über Nacht durch natürliche Querlüftung abgekühlt wurde, tagsüber länger kühl zu halten.

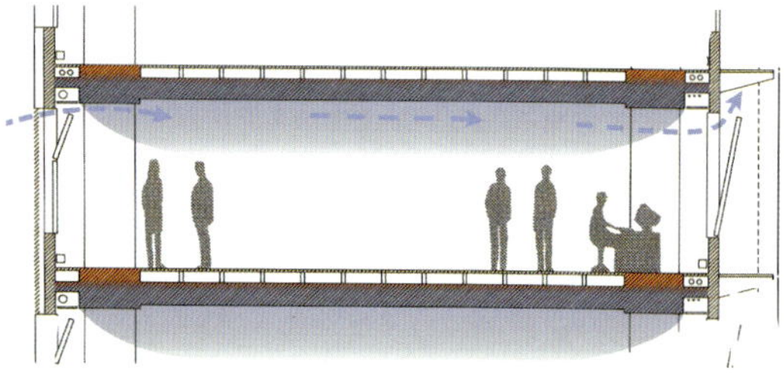

speichermasse - sommer thermal mass - summer

Thermal mass

The ceilings of the building remained generally uncovered so that the thermal mass of the primary structure can be used to condition internal temperatures. Particularly in summer the thermal capacity of the material is used to keep the building cool during the day, as it has been cooled down during the night (through cross-ventilation).

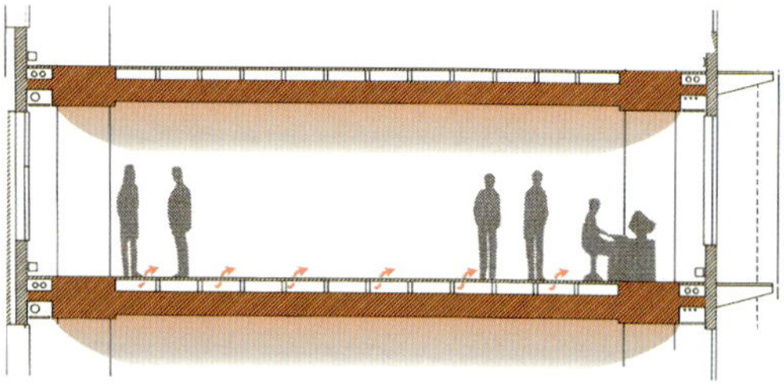

speichermasse - winter thermal mass - winter

Wärmerückgewinnung

Da im Winter die Aussenluft für natürliche Belüftung zu kühl bzw. der Wärmebedarf zur Heizung der Aussenluft zu hoch ist, wird für den Winter eine mechanische Lüftungsanlage vorgehalten, die das Gebäude zentral belüftet. Diese Lüftungsanlage erlaubt die Wiedergewinnung der Abluftwärme und senkt damit entsprechenden Heizbedarf.

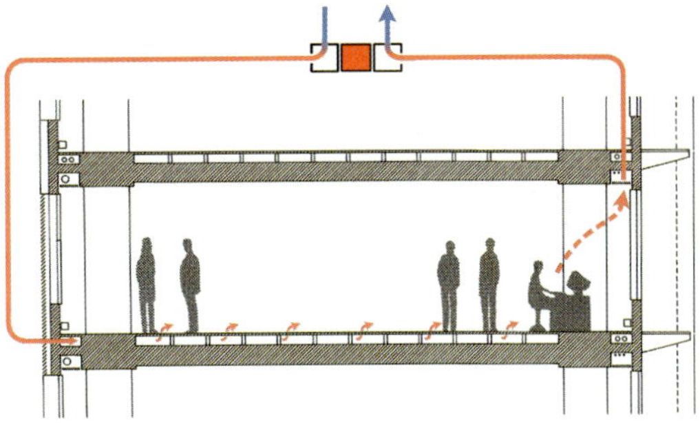

energierückgewinnung *energy regain*

Heat recovery

As the external air is too cold in the winter to effectively heat up incoming air, there is a mechanical system to ventilate the building during winter time. During this period exhaust air is pulled through an exchange system to preheat incoming fresh air.

Innenaufnahme Hochhaus vor dem Ausbau
View of the high-rise before interior fit-out

Deckenspiegel Hochhaus M. ca. 1:400
Reflected ceiling plan high-rise scale ca. 1:400

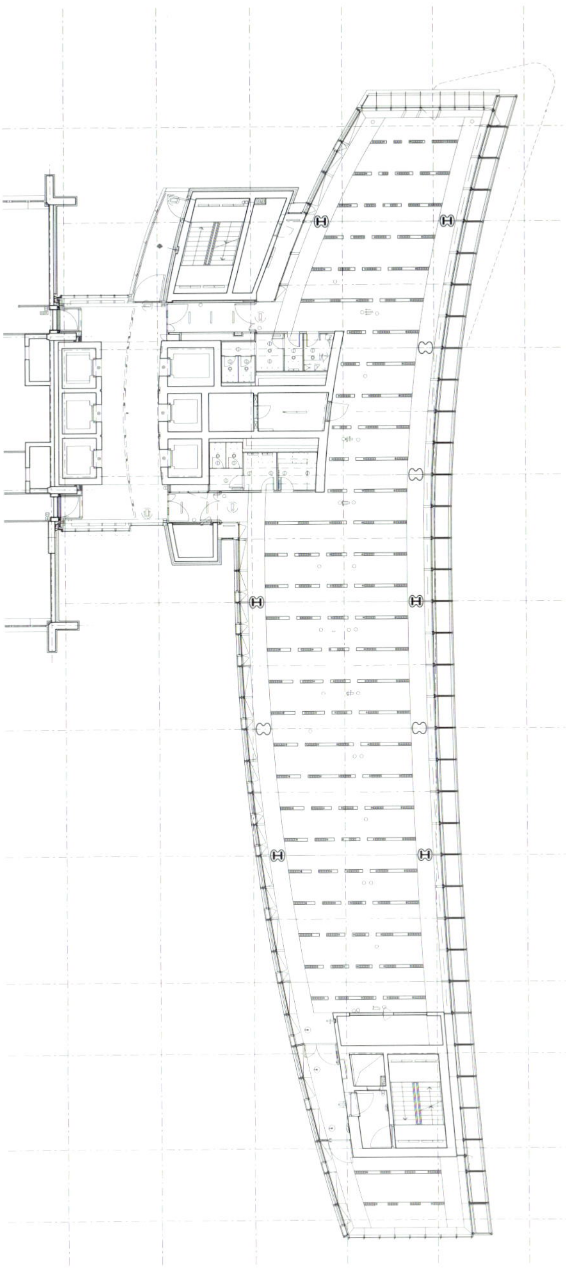

Winddach

Das sogenannte Winddach ist ein Gebäudeteil, der als direktes Resultat der Gebäudesimulation sowie der zwei Windkanaltests entstanden ist. Seine Aufgabe besteht darin, erstens wie ein Schirm die nach oben hin offene Konvektionsfassade vor dem Regen zu schützen und zweitens Windströme zu leiten.
Wenn der Wind aus westlichen Richtungen bläst (Hauptwindrichtung), wird er durch die Form des Daches direkt über die Oberkante der Abluftfassade geleitet. Durch das Profil des Daches wird der Wind beschleunigt und der Unterdruck in der Fassade erhöht (*Venturi*-Effekt), sodass deren natürliche Konvektionswirkung unterstützt wird.
Bläst der Wind in Längsrichtung des Gebäudes, wird der Luftstrom durch am Winddach angebrachte *Windflossen* verwirbelt und somit verhindert, dass durch Wind Überdrücke in der Fassade entstehen können.

Wind roof

**The wind roof is an element of the building which came into existence as a direct result of both the engineer's CFD simulations and the wind tunnel tests.
When the wind blows from the west (which is the main wind direction) it will be drawn directly over the top edge of the thermal flue. Due to the profile of the roof the wind accelerates so that the negative pressure in the flue will be increased (due to the so-called *Venturi* effect) reinforcing natural convection.
If the wind is blowing from northerly or southerly directions, a series of fins suspended over the flue cause the wind to eddy. This prevents the build-up of positive pressure in the flue.**

Vindströmungen an der Westfassade
Vind flow on the west façade

/lodelle für Windkanalversuch
/lodels for wind-tunnel tests

Entwurfszeichnungen Winddach

Design drawings wind roof

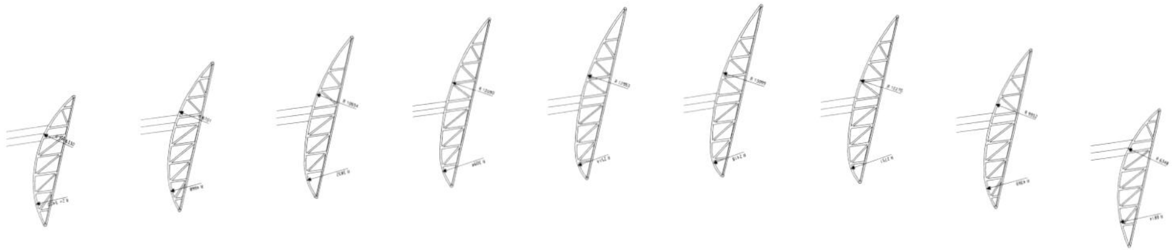

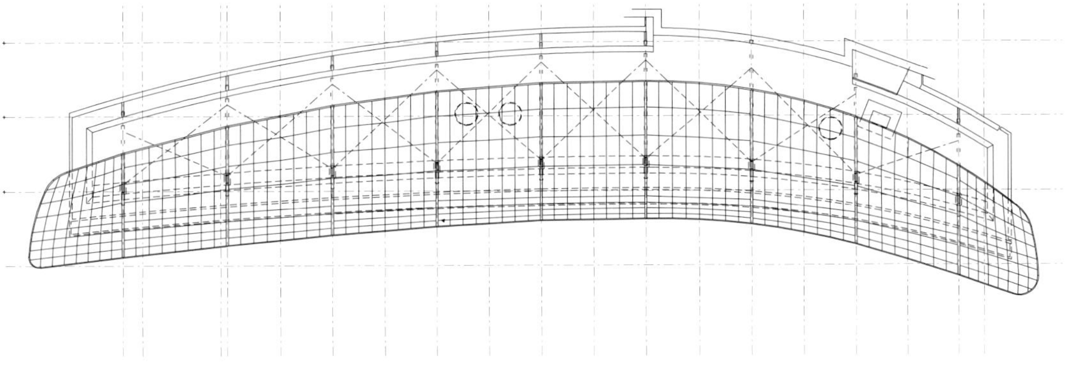

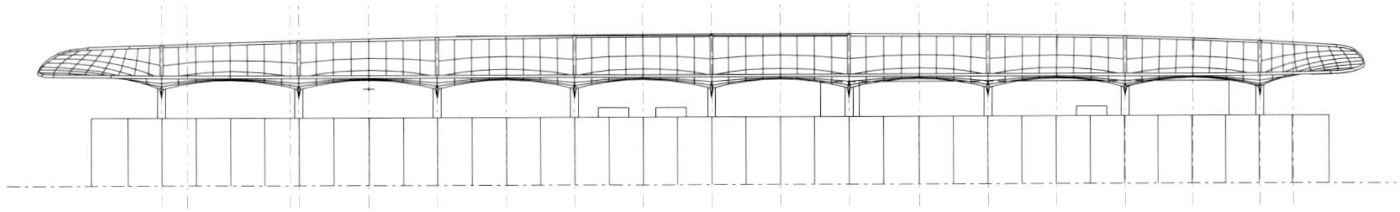

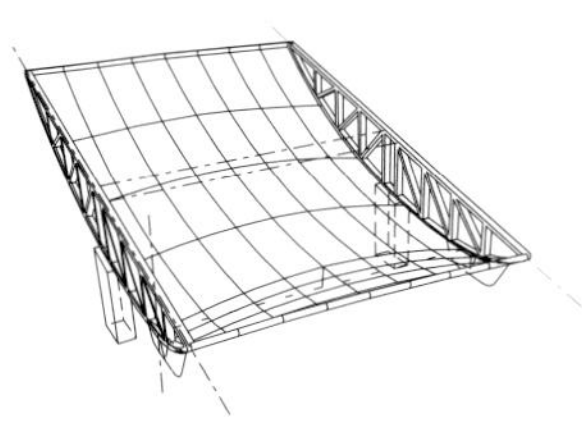

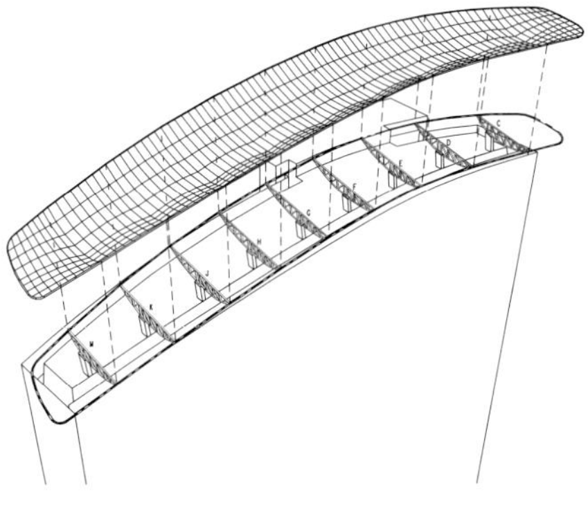

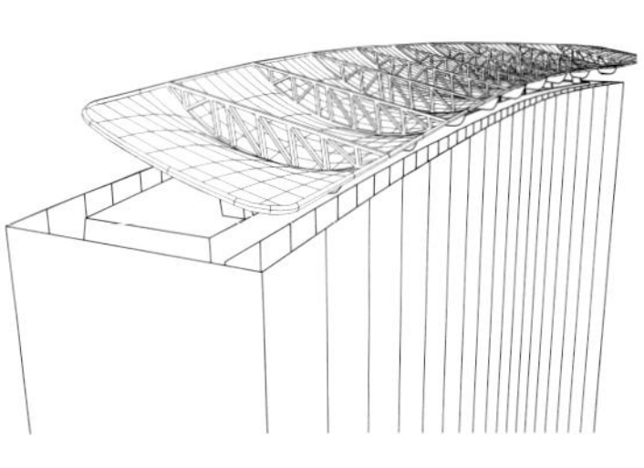

Fassaden

Die Hochhausfassaden sind die wichtigsten baulichen Elemente des Niedrigenergiekonzeptes. Ein hoher Glasanteil erlaubt maximale Tagesbelichtung. Über Sonnen- und Blendschutz werden Wärme- und Lichteinlass geregelt; durch Ausbildung von Pufferzonen in den doppelten Glasschichten verfügen sie über einen relativ hohen Transmissionswärmewiderstand. Die Ostfassade mit ihren porenhaften Zuluftöffnungen funktioniert wie eine glatte Haut; die Westfassade, mit ihrer Tiefe und der Auflösung in gestaffelte Schichten, gleicht einem Fell. Alle flexiblen Elemente der Fassade sind individuell von jedem Arbeitsplatz steuerbar und mit einem zentralen Steuerungssystem verbunden.

Façades

The high-rise façades are the most important elements of the low-energy concept. A high degree of transparency allows for maximum daylight. The transmission of heat and light into the interior is controlled through the use of solar shutters and blinds; the buffer zones of double-layer glass façades both east and west achieve high insulation values. The east façade with its porous ventilation openings is like a smooth skin, whereas the west façade-with its depth and separation into several layers - resembles a fur. All moveable elements of the façades are to be controlled by the individual occupant, but they can also be operated by a central building management system.

Westfassade

Die Westfassade der Hochhausscheibe ist aus drei Schichten aufgebaut: Die innerste Schicht besteht aus einer Aluminiumvorhangfassade mit Verglasung zwischen Decke und Brüstung, die in jeder zweiten Achse zu öffnen ist. An den Vertikalpfosten dieser inneren Fassade sind auskragende Stahlschwerter angebracht, die die äussere Fassadenschicht halten. Auf diesen Schwertern liegen Gitterroste auf, sodass der Fassadenzwischenraum begehbar ist. Die äussere Schicht besteht aus einer einfachen Verbundglasscheibe mit einer Grösse von 3,3 × 1,8 m, die im Gegensatz zu der elementierten Innenschicht vor Ort montiert wurde. Zwischen den Schichten befindet sich ein beweglicher Sonnenschutz aus 3,0 × 0,9 m grossen, perforierten Blechen. Diese Bleche sind per Motor schwenkbar und seitlich verschiebbar. Die Anordnung der farbigen Sonnenschutzläden hängt von den Gewohnheiten der Benutzer des Gebäudes ab, sodass die Westfassade ein sich ständig veränderndes Bild bietet. Der Konvektionsraum der Fassade ist oben und unten durch Klappen verschliessbar, sodass der Luftstrom je nach Witterungsbedingungen geregelt werden kann.

West façade

The west façade of the high-rise comprises three layers. The inner layer consists of a double-glazed aluminium curtain wall in which every second bay has an openable window. The vertical posts of this inner façade carry cantilevering brackets to support the outer façade. This layer is single-glazed, and consists of 3.3 × 1.8 m laminated glass panes which were mounted on site (as opposed to the elements of the inner façade which were prefabricated). The space between the two layers is accessible, as the brackets carry metal-mesh decking. The air flow within the inner and outer skins of the façade can be regulated according to weather conditions by dampers at the top and the bottom. Within the flue, shielded from the weather, lies the solar protection. This consists of 3.0 m × 0.9 m sized perforated metal shutters which can be both pivoted and moved aside mechanically. The patterns formed from these coloured shutters – and thus compositions of the whole façade – depends upon the habits of the occupants, so that the west façade offers an ever-changing image.

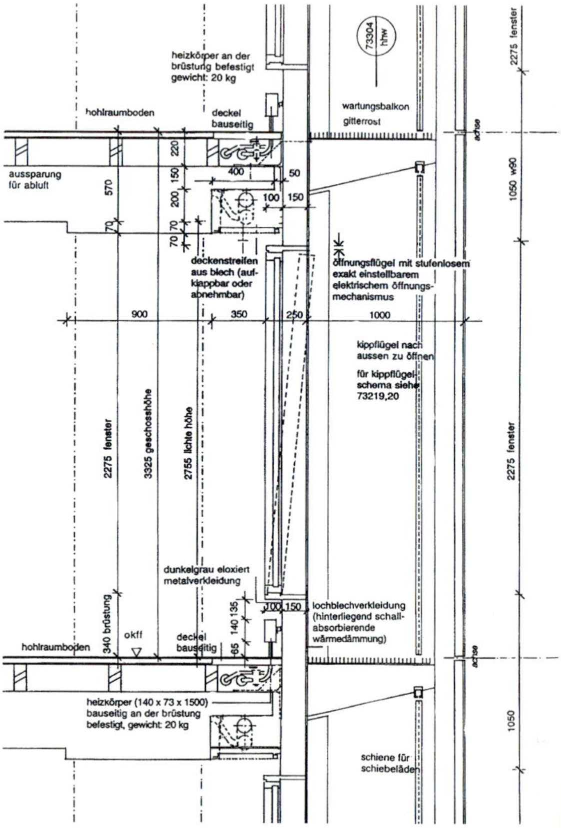

Prinzipschnitt Westfassade
Principle section west façade

Grundriss 19. Obergeschoss M. ca. 1:1000
19th floor plan scale ca. 1:1000

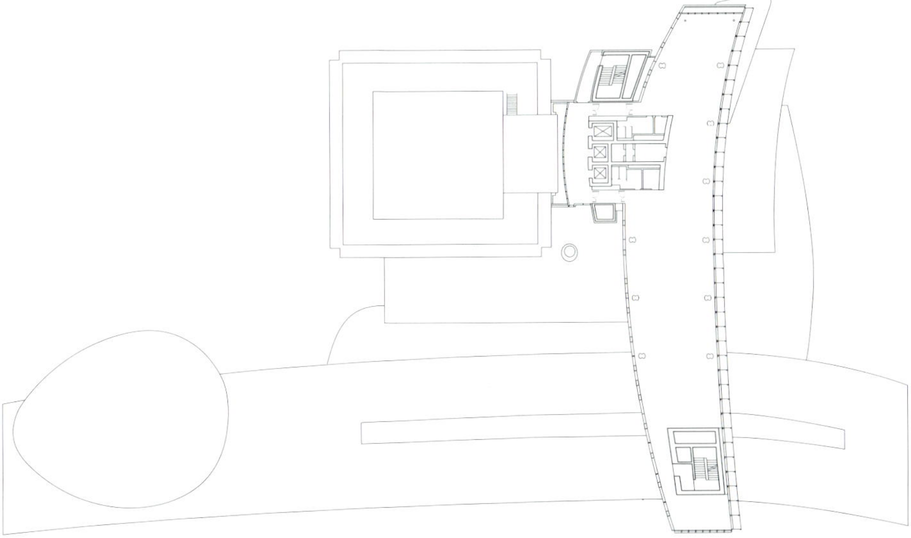

Nord- und Südfassade

Die Schmalseiten der Hochhausscheibe bilden die Schichtung des Gebäudes ab. Insbesondere an der Nordseite kann man den Streifen der Konvektionsfassade im Westen, die Raumzonen in der Mitte und die Zone der Ostfassade ablesen. Auch auf der Südseite bilden sich die Westfassade und die Raumzone deutlich ab. Die Vertikalität der beiden Fassaden wird durch die Struktur des feststehenden Sonnenschutzes im Süden sowie durch ein plastisch betontes Vertikalprofil auf der Nordseite hervorgehoben.

North and south façade

The narrow ends of the high-rise slab illustrate the layered plan of the building. Particularly on the north façade one can clearly detect the depth of the solar flue in the west, the office zone in the middle and the band of the east façade. Also on the south side, the west façade and the office zone are easily legible. The verticality of the two façades is emphasized in the south through a continuous field of fixed louvres and in the north through the narrow rhythm of especially articulated profiles.

Detailschnitt Westfassade

Detail section west façade

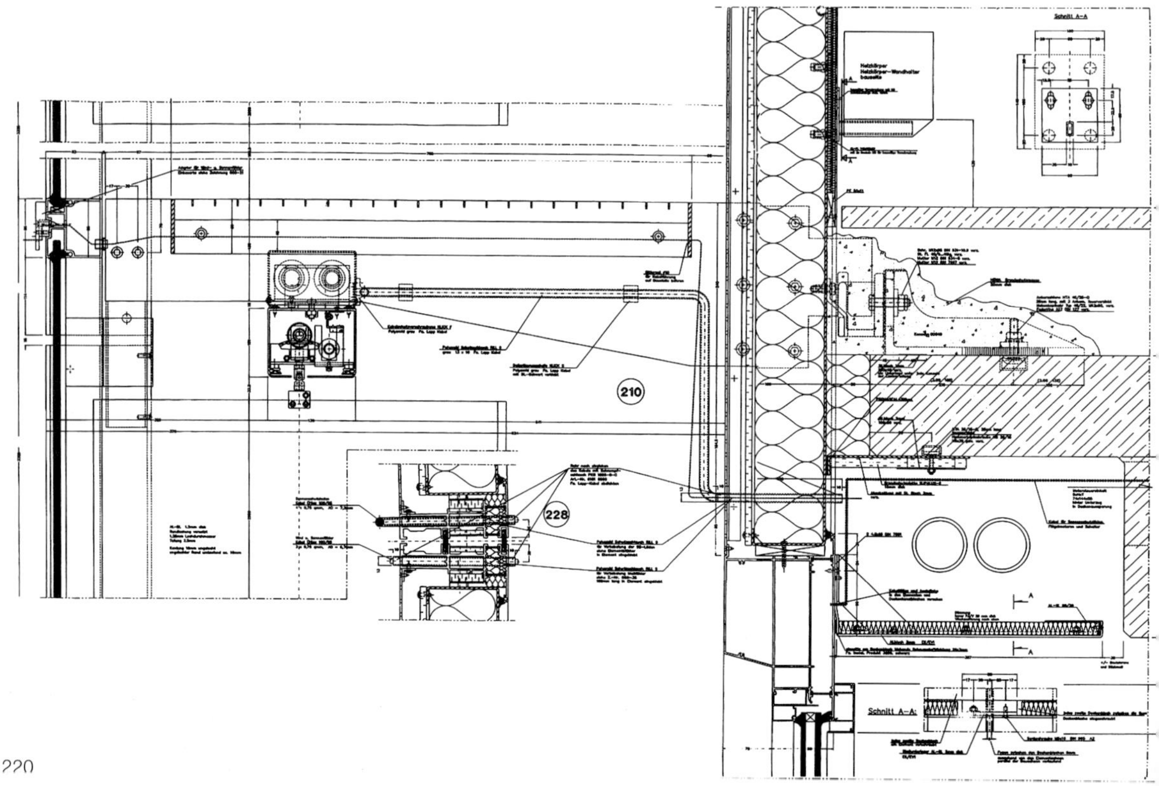

Ostfassade

Die Ostfassade ist die Zuluftfassade; hier tritt Luft über Lüftungsfelder in das Gebäude ein, die dann über den Konvektionsschacht der Westfassade wieder abgeführt wird. Diese Lüftungselemente sind aussen mit Lamellenblechen abgedeckt und innen über geschlossene Dreh- oder Kippflügel öffenbar. Sie sind so über die Fassade verteilt, dass eine Vielzahl von verschiedenen Möblierungsalternativen für die dahinterliegenden Bürogeschosse möglich ist.
Neben einer Lüftungsöffnung für jedes Büro sind auch zentrale Zuluftöffnungen vorgesehen, die bei zweihüftigen Grundrissen notwendig werden. So entsteht auch auf dieser Fassade ein der Nutzung entsprechendes, unregelmässiges Muster.
Zwischen den Lüftungsöffnungen befinden sich zweischichtige Glasfelder, die innen aus einem doppelverglasten Fensterelement bestehen (das zu Reinigungszwecken auch öffenbar ist) und aussen durch eine einfache VSG-Glasscheibe im Sicht- und weiss emaillierten Glas im Brüstungsbereich abgedeckt ist.
Diese äussere Schicht ist hinterlüftet, sodass zwischen den Fassadenschichten kein Wärmestau entstehen kann.
Gleichwohl bietet die Doppelfassade erhöhten Wärmeschutz und Windschatten für die zwischen den Schichten angeordneten Sonnenschutzlamellen.

East façade

The east façade is the façade for air intake. Here fresh air enters the building which will be extracted via the solar flue of the west façade. The openings for air intake are clad on the outside with louvres and are equipped with pivoting windows on the inside. These ventilation openings are distributed across the façade in such a way that a multitude of alternative office layouts for the different floors is possible. In addition to individual openings for every office there are central fresh air inlets which are necessary to ventilate double-banked layouts. This results in an asymmetrical composition of the louvres on the façade showing a direct relationship to the use of the building.
The rest of the façade is made of two layers of glass, with double-glazed windows on the inside (openable only for cleaning) and a single-glazed layer on the outside.
The space between is ventilated so that heat cannot become trapped. Nevertheless this façade offers very good thermal insulation, and in addition wind protection for the solar blinds lying within it's depth.

Prinzipschnitt Ostfassade
Principle section east façade

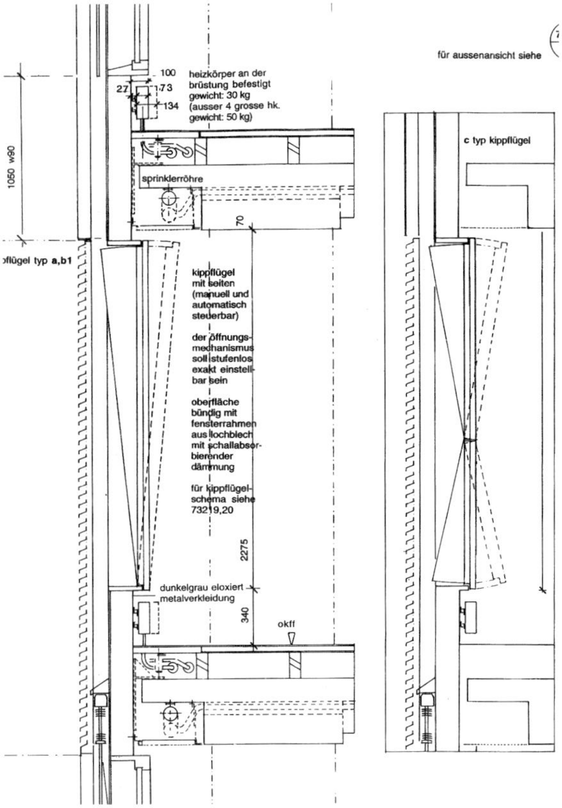

Detailschnitt Ostfassade durch Brüstung und Fenster

Detail section east façade through spandrel-panel and window

Detailschnitt Ostfassade durch Lüftungslamellen

Detail section east façade through ventilation louvres

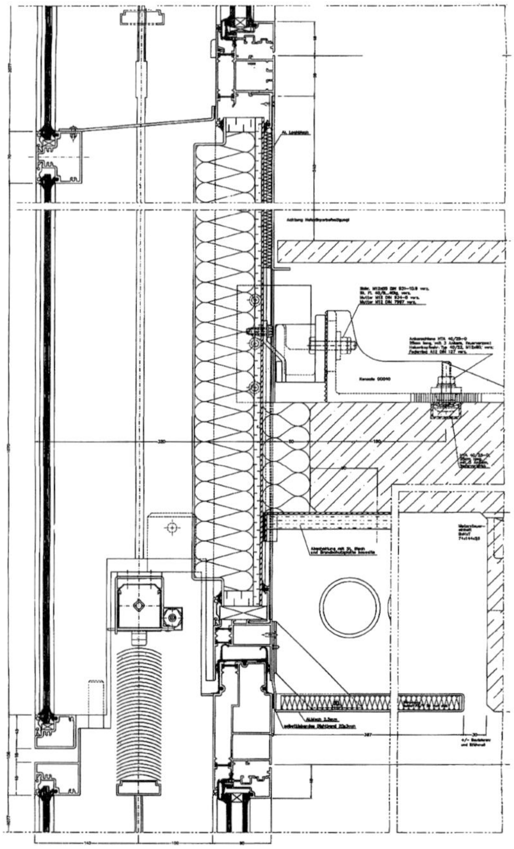

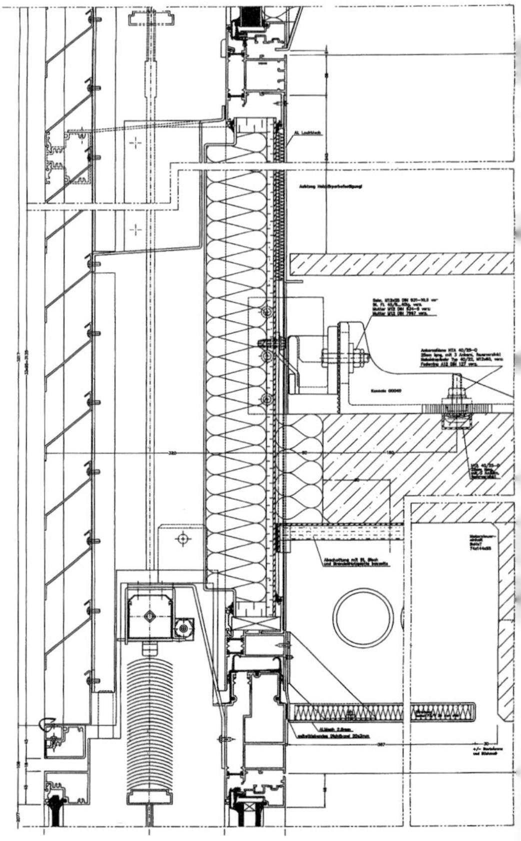

TAXI

ZÜBLIN
ZÜBLIN

Hans Jörg Duvigneau

GSW Gemeinnützige Siedlungs- und Wohnungsbaugesellschaft Berlin mbH

Zur Entwicklung des GSW-Hauses in der Kochstrasse

Die Etappen der GSW-Geschichte am Standort Kochstrasse in Berlin-Kreuzberg sind schnell aufgezählt:

Die grösste Wohnungsbaugesellschaft Berlins hatte durch Krieg und Teilung ihren Hauptsitz in Berlin-Mitte, Dorotheenstrasse, verloren. Seit 1949 auf ihren in den Westsektoren befindlichen Wohnungsbestand reduziert, war die Hauptverwaltung der GSW seit 1949 provisorisch am Grazer Damm in der ehemaligen Bauleitung mehr schlecht als recht untergebracht, bis man sich 10 Jahre später zu einem eigenen Neubau im Tiergartenviertel entschloss.

Auf Weisung des Landes Berlins musste das Projekt aufgegeben werden, um ein von der Stadt im traditionellen Zeitungsviertel für ganz andere Zwecke begonnenes Gebäude an der Kochstrasse zu vollenden und zu nutzen: Seit 1961 hat die GSW ihre Hauptverwaltung im Hochhaus der Architekten Schwebes, Schoszberger und Noth, Kochstrasse 22.

Bis in die 80er Jahre hatte die GSW in Berlin (-West) ihren Wohnungsbestand auf 54 000 Wohnungen fast verdoppelt. In gleichem Umfang wuchsen die Verwaltungsaufgaben. Die räumlichen Kapazitäten im Turmbau an der Kochstrasse waren erschöpft, eine Erweiterung wurde erforderlich.

Mit dem Architekten Helge Pitz entwickelte die GSW ein Projekt, das die für das Unternehmen notwendige Erweiterung mit *Stadtreparatur* und der Wiederherstellung des historischen Stadtraums an der Kochstrasse, Charlottenstrasse und Markgrafenstrasse zu verbinden erlaubte – ganz im Sinne der Ziele der Internationalen Bauausstellung: Das Projekt sah eine 6- bis 7-geschossige, strassenparallele Randbebauung vor, mit der die traditionelle Berliner Traufhöhe erreicht wurde, wie sie die im Krieg nicht untergegangenen Bürohäuser in der Umgebung zeigten, die ja *massgeblich* wurden für die unter IBA-Regie in den 80er-Jahren in der Kochstrasse und Friedrichstrasse geschaffenen Neubauten von Rossi, Eisenman, Bohigas, Zenghelis/Sauerbruch, Kammerer/Belz und Spangenberg.

Zunächst wurde in den späten 80er mit Umbaumassnahmen im und am Turmgebäude begonnen, wie der Erweiterung der Eingangshalle, dem Ausbau des Mieterberatungszentrums im 1. OG, eines Versammlungsraumes und des Mitarbeiterrestaurants im 16. OG.

Die Genehmigung des eigentlichen Erweiterungsprojekts scheiterte an kleinkarierten Bedenken des Bezirks Kreuzberg und der Senatsverwaltung für Stadtentwicklung und Umweltschutz: Bei den Verwaltungen gab es damals kein Verständnis für den Erweiterungsbedarf der GSW, erst recht nicht die Bereitschaft, für solche Zwecke die Verlegenheitsgrünfläche entlang der Kochstrasse zu opfern, die einst als Vorratsfläche für den Bau einer Stadtautobahn in städtisches Eigentum erworben worden war. Trotz des geringen Werts dieser verlärmten, zugigen, von Hundeexkrementen verschmutzten Grünanlage hielt man an ihrer Erhaltung fest.

Die GSW war gezwungen, für viele Jahre Büroräume in der Nachbarschaft anzumieten und ihren Kunden und Mitarbeitern die damit verbundenen Unbequemlichkeiten zuzumuten.

Hans Jörg Duvigneau
GSW Gemeinnützige Siedlungs- und Wohnungsbaugesellschaft Berlin mbH

On the Development of the GSW Headquarters in Kochstrasse

The various stages of GSW's history on it's site at Kochstrasse in Berlin's Borough of Kreuzberg are easily recounted:

The city's largest Housing Association had lost it's main headquarters in Dorotheenstrasse, central Berlin, through the separation of the city after the war. From 1949 GSW's housing stock had been reduced to that which happened to be located in the western sector of Berlin. It's headquarters were located provisionally (and unsatisfactorily) at Grazer Damm in a building which had formerly been used for the supervision of a building site, until – 10 years later – the decision was taken eventually to build a new building in the district of Tiergarten.

At the request of the City Council this project had to be abandoned, in order to complete and bring into use a building in the traditional press quarter which had been built with a completely different purpose in mind. Since 1961 GSW has had it's headquarters in the high-rise building at Kochstrasse 22, designed by the architects Schwebes, Schoszberger und Noth.

By the eighties GSW had virtually doubled it's housing stock to 54,000 (in West Berlin). The administrative requirements had grown at the same rate. The spatial capacity of the tower on Kochstrasse had reached it's limit and an extension became a matter of necessity.

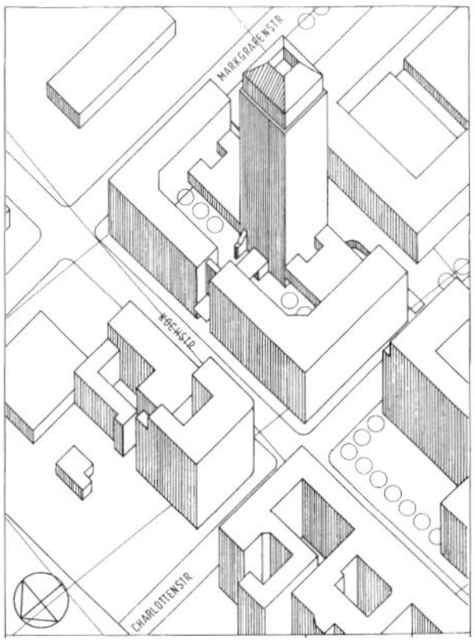

GSW developed a project with the architects Helge Pitz which fulfilled both the clients' need for extension and, at the time, ideas of *City Repair* and the reinstatement of the historical streetscape at Kochtrasse, Charlottenstrasse and Markgrafenstrasse – compatible with the intentions of the International Building Exhibition 1984 (IBA). Proposed was a 6 to 7 storey building parallel to the street, which could make reference to the traditional cornice height of Berlin – still apparent on a few office buildings in the neighbourhood which survived the war – and which had become the yardstick for buildings designed under the aegis of IBA along Kochstrasse and Friedrichstrasse by Rossi, Eisenmann, Bohigas, Zenghelis/Sauerbruch, Kammerer/Belz and Spangenberg.

First renovations in and around the tower had been completed during the eighties such as the extension of the entrance hall, the relocation of the tenants' advice centre on the first floor and the renovation of a meeting room and the canteen on the 16th floor.

The permission for the extension itself foundered due to the small-minded reservations of the Borough of Kreuzberg and of the Senate for Urban Development and the Environment. In the administration at that time there was no understanding of GSW's need for extension – not even the readiness to sacrifice an embarassing strip of land along Kochstrasse – which had become the property of the city having been set aside for the construction of a drastically widened street.

Georg Wittwer, Bausenator von 1986 bis 1989, gab unmittelbar nach dem gescheiterten Vorbescheidsverfahren den Anstoss für einen neuen Anlauf. Auf seinen Vorschlag wurde ein Realisierungswettbewerb mit beschränkter Teilnehmerzahl vorbereitet, der eine verbindliche Klärung der offen gebliebenen Fragen herbeiführen sollte. Paradoxerweise wurde in Abstimmung zwischen allen beteiligten Verwaltungen die gerade verworfene Blockrandbebauung zur verpflichtenden Vorgabe aller Teilnehmer.
1990, ein halbes Jahr nach der Wende, wurde der Wettbewerb unter Bausenator Wolfgang Nagel dann abgehalten.

Folgende Architekturbüros arbeiteten an dem Projekt:
Brenner/Thonon
Langhof
Nägeli/Vallebuona
Oestreich/Henschel
Sauerbruch
Spangenberg

Der Jury gehörten an:
Hildebrand Machleidt, Architekt BDA, Vorsitzender
Prof. Hans Kollhoff, Architekt BDA
Hilde Léon, Architektin BDA
Helge Pitz, Architekt BDA
und Klaus Keller, Ltd. Baudirektor, Senatsverwaltung für Bau- und Wohnungswesen
Günter König, Bezirksbürgermeister von Kreuzberg
Hans Jörg Duvigneau, Architekt, Geschäftsführer GSW

Die Jury hat sich angesichts der eingereichten Entwürfe noch einmal intensiv mit der Aufgabenstellung und den städtebaulichen Vorgaben für den Standort auseinandergesetzt. Im Protokoll der Preisgerichtssitzung am 11. Dezember 1990 heisst es dazu:

... «Die Einhaltung der IBA-Forderung, in der südlichen Friedrichstadt die Traufhöhen der Gründerzeit als Massstab für den Stadtraum zu respektieren, führt im Fall der GSW-Erweiterung nur bedingt zu tauglichen städtebaulichen Lösungen: Typologische Konzepte der 50er-Jahre wie das Graphische, und Gewerbezentrum mit dem GSW-Hochhaus oder der Springer-Komplex gegenüber, lassen sich nicht durch Ergänzungen mit einem anderen typologischen Repertoire *korrigieren*.

Insbesondere bei den Lösungen, die das GSW-Hochhaus aus seiner asymmetrischen Position in die Mitte eines neuen, nun symmetrischen Raumes stellen, zeigt sich als Problem, dass sich die Architektur des Hochhauses für eine zentrale Position im Grunde nicht eignet. Prinzipiell richtiger erscheinen daher alle Lösungen, die mit einer freien städtebaulichen Komposition dem Raum eine neue Ordnung zu geben versuchen.»

Die Jury kommt schliesslich zu dem Ergebnis, zwei Erste Preise zu vergeben:

Zum Entwurf Brenner/Thonon sagt die Jury (Auszüge):
«Der Entwurf macht sich das Thema der Symmetrie zu eigen, ohne dabei das Hochhaus zu monumentalisieren.

In spite of the trivial value of this noisy, drafty, and dog-excrement-defiled strip of grass the authorities stuck fast to their position.

GSW was forced for many years to rent offices in the surrounding area, and it's employees and clients had to endure the resulting inconvenience.

Georg Wittwer, Senator for Building from 1986–1989, initiated the next step immediately after the first planning application had failed. On his suggestion a competition with a limited number of invited participants was organised – with the aim of resolving all the open questions. Paradoxically, all the parties who had previously been involved now agreed that the recently-rejected perimeter block solution should in fact form the urban model for the competitors. In 1990, half a year after the Reunification, the competition was held under the auspices of Building Senator Wolfgang Nagel.

The following architects' offices were invited:
Brenner/Thonon
Langhof
Nägeli/Vallebuona
Oestreich/Henschel
Sauerbruch
Spangenberg

The members of the Jury were:
Hildebrandt Machleidt, architect BDA, Chairman
Prof. Hans Kolhoff, architect BDA
Hilde Léon, architect BDA
Helge Pitz, architect BDA
as well as
Klaus Keller, Director of the Senate's Dept. for Building and Housing
Günter König, Mayor of Kreuzberg
Hans Jörg Duvigneau, architect, Managing Director of GSW

When confronted with the actual designs submitted, the jury thoroughly discussed the brief and its urban considerations once again. The minutes of the meeting on 11 December 1990 state:

... "The IBA concept to respect the cornice height of the 19C blocks as the reference for the urban space in southern Friedrichstadt leads, in the case of the GSW extension, only partially to acceptable solutions. Typological concepts from the '50s such as the GGZ together with the GSW high-rise, or the Springer complex opposite, cannot be *corrected* through additions from another typological repertoire.

In particular those proposals which set the currently asymmetrical GSW tower in the centre of a new symmetrical space demonstrate the fact that this high-rise is basically not suited to a centralised position. Those proposals which try to use free urban compositions to create a new order seem more correct."

The jury finally came to the conclusion that they should award two first prizes:

Unzureichend gelöst ist die Verbindung von GSW-Hochhaus zu dem Baukörper in der Charlottenstrasse. Die Lage der Zugänge der Gebäude an den Seitenstrassen wird kritisch gesehen. Gesucht werden sollte die Kochstrasse als *Adresse*.»

Den Entwurf Sauerbruch beurteilt die Jury wie folgt (Auszüge):
«Der Entwurf bietet funktional die beste Erfüllung des Programms, soweit es die Verbindung des GSW-Hochhauses mit dem Erweiterungsbau betrifft.

Die vorgeschlagene Hochhausscheibe ist eine souveräne und originelle Lösung für das Problem der baulichen Ergänzung des Bautyps des Graphischen und Gewerbezentrums mit dem GSW-Hochhaus. Die danebengestellte Hochhausscheibe erklärt sich … dem GSW-Hochhaus zugehörig, ohne dabei auf einen eigenen architektonischen Ausdruck zu verzichten. Es entsteht auf diese Weise ein neues Ensemble, in dem freilich das neue Element dominiert.

Sehr gut gelöst ist der Zugang zu den Hochhäusern über eine gemeinsame Halle, die sich aus der Bürohauszeile an der Kochstrasse in die Tiefe des Grundstückes entwickelt. Den Bedenken vor möglicherweise hohen Kosten des Projekts stehen gegenüber
– die funktionalen Qualitäten der Verbindung der Gebäude (Rationalisierungseffekt)
– das starke Image des Gebäudes als Sitz der GSW,
– das grosse Angebot an sofort realisierbarer Nutzfläche ohne Abhängigkeit von einem zweiten Bauabschnitt.»

Das Preisgericht empfiehlt eine Weiterentwicklung der beiden erstplatzierten Entwürfe und formuliert für diese Überarbeitung eine Reihe konkreter Prüfaufträge.

In einer vergleichenden Analyse stellte sich heraus, dass wegen der in beiden Entwürfen gleichermassen erforderlichen hohen Aufwendungen für Gründung und Stellplätze kaum nennenswerte Kostenunterschiede erkennbar waren, dass aber bei Kostengleichheit die *inneren Werte* des Entwurfs Sauerbruch desto deutlicher hervortraten, eben die vom Preisgericht bereits herausgearbeiteten konzeptionellen Qualitäten:
– Konzentration des gesamten neuen Bauvolumens in einem ersten Bauabschnitt;
– Verbindung des bestehenden und neuen Bürohauses auf jeder Ebene;
– hinzu kam die bestechende Idee für das Klimakonzept des neuen Hochhauses, das auf dem einfachen Prinzip der Querlüftung basiert.

Die GSW-Geschäftsführung entschied sich daher im Frühjahr 1991 für den Entwurf Sauerbruch; der Aufsichtsrat billigte diese Entscheidung, das Preisgericht nahm diese Entscheidung mit Befriedigung zur Kenntnis.

Jedoch war nicht vorherzusehen, dass das Baugenehmigungsverfahren für das von Senatsbauverwaltung, Bezirk und GSW gemeinsam gewollte Projekt sich über mehr als vier Jahre erstrecken würde. Die im 1. Quartal 1991 neu berufene Stadtbaurätin im Bezirksamt Kreuzberg, eine erklärte Hochhausgegnerin, bot alle Mittel auf, um das Vorhaben zu verhindern. Erst durch die Entscheidungen der Senatsbauverwaltung wurde dem Widerspruch der GSW gegen die Ablehnung des Vorbescheidsantrags stattgegeben. Im Frühjahr 1995 wurden dank der konstruktiven Mitarbeit in den beteiligten Ämtern

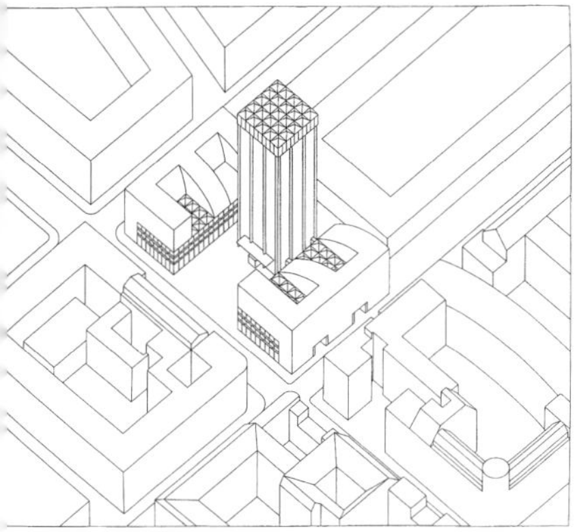

Concerning the scheme by Brenner/Tonon the jury commented (extract):

"Although the design uses symmetry as it's theme, this does not turn the high-rise into a monument.
The connection of the GSW high-rise with the building along Charlottenstrasse is not sufficiently resolved.

The positioning of main entrances on the side streets is criticised. One should try to make... Kochstrasse the address."

The jury judged Sauerbruch's design as follows (extract):
"The design offers the best response to the brief, as far as the connection of the GSW tower with the extension is concerned.

The proposed high-rise slab is an ingenious and original solution to the brief of an extension to the building type of the GGZ with the GSW high-rise. The adjacent high-rise slab associates itself... with the GSW tower, without losing its own architectural expression. In this way a new ensemble is created in which – of course – the new slab is the dominant element.

The access to the high-rises is very well resolved with a common entrance hall which leads one from the office building along Kochstrasse into the depth of the site. The reservations about possible high costs are to be seen in the light of:
- the functional quality of the connection of the buildings (operational efficiency)
- the strong image of the building as the headquarters of GSW
- the opportunity to realize a large amount of office space immediately, independent of a second building phase."

The jury recommended that both premiated schemes are reworked, and formulated a series of questions for this revision.

In a comparative study it was shown that both designs needed similar expenditure for foundations and the creation of underground parking. However, given comparable cost, the *internal values* of the Sauerbruch design stood out even more clearly in their conceptual qualities which the jury had already recognised:
- the concentration of the complete area required in an initial building phase
- the connection of the existing to the new office building on every level
- in addition there was the convincing idea for the environmental concept of the new high-rise based on the simple principle of cross ventilation.

So the management of GSW decided for Sauerbruch's design in Spring 1991, the board seconded this decision to the satisfaction of the Jury.

What could not have been foreseen was that it would take more than four years to obtain the planning permission for this project which had the joint support of the Senate, the Borough and GSW.

des Bezirks die ersten Teilbaugenehmigungen erteilt; im Juni 1995 konnte mit der Grundsteinlegung der eigentliche Baubeginn erfolgen.

Die bauliche Realisierung des Projekts wurde durch eine Vielzahl von Problemen beeinträchtigt. Der schwierige Baugrund verlangte tiefe Pfahlgründungen; ein Wassereinbruch im Tiefkeller des automatischen Tiefparksystems hatte einen mehrmonatigen Baustopp zur Folge. Unregelmässige Mitnahmesetzungen führten beim Bau der Hochhausfundamente zu einer Schiefstellung des Altbaus, der mit aufwändiger Hochdruckinjektionstechnik behoben werden musste. Bei diesen Arbeiten wurde de gesamte Altbau um 3 cm angehoben! Schliesslich wurden noch alte Maschinenfundamente im Bereich unter dem ehemaligen Druckereigebäude gefunden, sodass sich die Arbeiten im Tiefbaubereich um insgesamt ein Jahr verzögerten. Gerade in diesen schwierigen Phasen, aber auch bei der Findung des Haupttragwerks sowie bei der Umsetzung des innovativen Klimakonzeptes haben das Planungsteam und die Bauleitung in engster Zusammenarbeit mit den Baufirmen Lösungen für die auftretenden Realisierungsprobleme entwickelt und baureif gemacht.

Der Einzug in das neue Gebäude erfolgte im Juli 1999. In jenem Sommer mit einer ungewöhnlich langen Schönwetterperiode und den über viele Wochen anhaltenden hohen Temperaturen hat das Klimasystem des Hauses seine Bewährungsprobe erfolgreich bestanden: Die durch den Auftrieb im Luftraum der Westfassade bewirkte Querlüftung erzeugte ein zugfreies, angenehmes Klima in den neuen Räumen, die Sonnenschutzlamellen erzeugten ein angenehmes, individuell steuerbares Licht.

Die GSW nutzt mit ihren Tochtergesellschaften mehr als zwei Drittel des Gesamtkomplexes. Seit 1999 sind weitere Nutzer als Mieter im Haus. Bis Ende 2000 werden die noch freien Flächen im Flachbau und in den oberen Geschossen der Hochhausscheibe vermietet sein.

Der Bauherr hat allen Anlass, mit diesem Werk zufrieden zu sein: Zunächst bietet der neue Gebäudekomplex genügend Raum für ein modernes Dienstleistungsunternehmen mit seinen PC-gestützten Arbeitsplätzen, seiner Teamarbeit, seiner Kundenorientierung und Weltoffenheit. Besonders freut uns die wohlwollende, oft begeisterte, immer anerkennende Akzeptanz der Gestalt des Hauses in den Medien, in der Fachwelt und beim Berliner Publikum.

In einer Zeit entspannter Wohnungsmärkte spielt der Wiedererkennungswert eines auf die Qualität seiner Dienstleistung bedachten grossen Vermieters auch eine Rolle. Ich freue mich darüber, dass die GSW mit diesem ungewöhnlichen Haus hierzu einen Beitrag leistet. Aber darüber hinaus wird das Haus auch als Bereicherung für das Stadtbild dieses Teils Berlins und als gelungenes Beispiel ökologischen Bauens empfunden und beschrieben.

Ich bin glücklich und erleichtert über die freundliche Aufnahme dieses Bauwerks in der Berliner Öffentlichkeit. Ich bin dankbar dafür, dass aus dem Zusammenwirken so vieler Beteiligter ein offenbar geglücktes Werk hervorgegangen ist. Ich wünsche mir, dass dieses Haus viele Jahre und Jahrzehnte der zentrale Ort für ein erfolgreiches Wirken der GSW bleiben möge, auch bei veränderter Gesellschafterkonstellation.

Berlin, 30. März 2000

A newly appointed head of the planning department – a declared enemy of high-rise buildings- used every possible means to boycott the project. Finally GSW's appeal against the refusal of planning permission was ratified by the Senator of Building. In Spring 1995 – thanks to the constructive collaboration of the involved departments of the Borough, the first partial building permit were issued. Finally – in June 1995 the building site could begin with the foundation stone ceremony.

The construction process was hampered by a number of problems. The difficult ground conditions made it necessary to build deep pile foundations; a leak in the caisson of the mechanical parking garage resulted in an interruption of construction for several months; uneven settlement of the new and the old building (when foundations were made) led to an incline of the existing tower, which had to be corrected with complicated high-pressure injection technology. (With this process the whole of the old building was raised by 3 cm!) Finally, old foundations underneath the former printing works had to be removed, so that the works below ground were delayed by a total of one year. It was particularly in those difficult phases, but also in the final definition of the structural system of the high-rise and in the realisation of the innovative environmental concept that the design team and the site agents developed and perfected solutions in very close collaboration with the contractors.

The building started to be occupied in July 1999. In this summer with its several week-long periods of sunny and hot weather the environmental system proved to be working: the convection caused by the solar flue on the west façade created a draft-free and fresh environment for the new offices and the solar shutters guaranteed pleasant and easily controlled daylight.

GSW and its subsidaries are using more than two thirds of the whole complex. Since 1999 there are also tenants in the building. All lettable areas in the upper floors of the high-rise slab will be let by the end of 2000.

The client has all reasons to be satisfied with this work. First of all the building complex offers suitable space for a modern service industry with its computer-aided workplaces, its teamwork, its client orientation and its international interests.

We were particularly happy with the design's sometimes enthusiastic and always positive reception in the media, the professional world and the Berlin public.

In a time of fierce competition the identity of a housing provider concerned with the quality of its service plays an important role. I am glad that GSW is contributing to such an image with this unusual project. In addition the building is seen as an improvement to this part of Berlin and has been described as a successful example of ecological building.

I am happy and relieved with the friendly reception of this building in Berlin. I am thankful that the collaboration of so many contributors has yielded an apparently successful work. I hope that this building may be the central location for the successful operation of GSW in many years – even if the structure of GSW itself may undergo changes.

Berlin, 30th March 2000

BECK

Bruttogeschossflächen und Bruttorauminhalt/Gross area and volumes

Gesamt/Total	181 912 BRI m^3	47 873 BGF m^2
Altbau/Existing tower	38 027 BRI m^3	11 837 BGF m^2
Neubau/New buildings	143 885 BRI m^3	36 036 BGF m^2
Eingangshalle/Entrance hall	3 697 BRI m^3	796 BGF m^2
Flachbau/Baguette	20 733 BRI m^3	5 873 BGF m^2
Baguettini	7 301 BRI m^3	1753 BGF m^2
Pillbox	5 132 BRI m^3	1 264 BGF m^2
Hochhaus/High-rise	60 041 BRI m^3	16 208 BGF m^2
Tiefgarage/Parking	46 981 BRI m^3	10 142 BGF m^2

Daten Baustelle und Gebäude/Building data

Baugrube/Excavation

Gebäude/Building	25 200 m^3	~ 6.300 $m^2 \times 4$ m (Tiefe/depth)
MPS/Mechanical parking system	19 000 m^3	~ 20 m × 50 m × 18 m (Tiefe/depth)
Berliner Verbau/Retaining walls	1900 m^2	~ 500 lfd. m
Wasserentnahme/Pumped ground water	1 Mio m^3	

Stabilisierung des alten Hochhauses/Stabilisation of the existing high-rise

Unterfangung/Underpinning

Hochdruckinjektionsmaterial/ High pressure injection material	386 t

Bohrpfahlgründung/Pile foundations

Flachbau/Baguette	35 Stck.	21,6 m (757,30 m)	Ø 0,90 m
Hochhaus/High-rise	67 Stck.	39,2 m (2 627,30 m)	Ø 1,20 m
	105 Stck.	7,5 m (787,50 m)	Ø 1,20 m

Verbauter Beton/Concrete used	15 000 m^3
Verbauter Stahl/Steel used	4 200 t
Höhe des Gebäudes/Building height	80,38 m
Baukosten/Building costs	160 Mio DM

AXEL SPRINGER VERLAG WELT

Beteiligte Firmen
Suppliers

Erdarbeiten und Baugrube/Excavation
ARGE Baugrube, Fa. Züblin/Bilfinger und Berger, Berlin

Bohrarbeiten und Wasserhaltung/Piling and foundations
Dankwart Klein, Berlin

Beton- und Stahlbetonarbeiten/Main structural contractors
ARGE Rohbau, Fa. Züblin/Bilfinger und Berger, Berlin

Fassaden- und Metallbauarbeiten/Façades and windows
Götz GmbH, Ludwigsburg

Fassaden/Façades
Gefatec, Gesellschaft für Fassadentechnik mbH, Berlin
Eternit Aktiengesellschaft, Berlin
Dach und Wand, Berlin

Stahlbau/Steel structure
Stahl- und Verbundbau Ges. f. industrielles Bauen mbH, Berlin

Winddach/Membrane roof
Koch Hightex, Rimsting

Schlosserarbeiten/Metal works
Hilse u. Wiehler GmbH, Alzey, Rheinhessen

Mechanisches Parksystem/Mechanical parksystem
Wöhr + Bauer GmbH, München

Holzarbeiten/Joinery
VHB Vereinigte Holzbaubetriebe GmbH, Memmingen
BKF Möbel u. Innenausbau GmbH, Berlin
G. Dallmann GmbH, Berlin

Dachdichtungen/Roofs
Wilhelm Brunzel GmbH, Heidelberg/Berlin
Blumenhügel Systeme GmbH, Alzenau
Wilbru, Wilhelm Brunzel GmbH, Heidelberg

Estricharbeiten/Screeds
Sari GmbH, Hanau
Roeder & Stockhorst GmbH, Mühlenbeck

Fliesenarbeiten/Floor and wall tiles
Turn Key Baugesellschaft mbH, Berlin

Malerarbeiten/Wall finishes
Westphal GmbH, Berlin

Trockenbau/Drywall construction
Trockenbau Gevelsberg GmbH, Gevelsberg
Westphal GmbH, Berlin

Sanitärtrennwände/WC partitions
Trennwand Stammberger, Berlin

Bürotrennwände/Office partitions
Mäder Schrank- und Trennwandsysteme, Dornstetten
Fischer Glas Technik, Hoppegarten

Hohlraumböden/Raised floor systems
Goldbach/Lindner Bodensysteme GmbH, Bergheim/Leipzig

Natursteinarbeiten/Natural stone floors
Marmor-Industrie Kiefer GmbH, Kiefersfelden

Beton- und Natursteinarbeiten/Stone and concrete floors
Gustav Popp Beton- u. Naturstein GmbH & Co. KG, Berlin

Fussbodenbeläge/Floor finishes
Wilhelm Dressel Fussboden GmbH, München

Parkett/Parquet floors
Bodentechnik Kretzschmar, Heidenau

Türen/Doors
Heinrich Spiess KG, Hof/Bayern

Brandschutztüren und -tore/Fire doors
Heinrich Spiess KG, Hof, Bayern
Hilse u. Wiehler GmbH, Alzey, Rheinhessen

Isolierung/Insulation
Licutherm Dämmtechnik GmbH, Berlin

Heizung/Heating
Insta GmbH, Projektion und Ausführung, Berlin
BHT Burckhardt Heizungstechnik, Berlin

Elektroarbeiten/Electrical equipment
Haase, Schalt- und Steuerungsanlagen, Brüsewitz
Elektrobau Peter Schulze GmbH, Berlin

Beleuchtung/Lighting
Ratio Licht GmbH, Neubiberg/Mülheim

Notstromanlage/Emergency power supply
Aggreko Deutschland GmbH

Sanitär- und Lüftungsinstallation/Sanitary and ventilation
Bolwin & Heemann, Anlagenbau, Bielefeld/Berlin

Sprinkleranlage/Sprinkler systems
Kraftanlagen Anlagentechnik Hamburg GmbH, Hamburg

Aufzugs- und Förderanlagen/Lifts
Koch-Aufzüge, Hamburg
Selzer-Aufzüge GmbH, Berlin
Schindler, Berlin

Fernmeldetechnik/Telecommunication
Alcatel/SEL AG, Berlin

Fernmelde-, Sicherheitstechnik/Information technology
Alstom AT GmbH, Berlin

Sicherheitstechnik/Security equipment
Garny GmbH, Hamburg/Berlin
Treder, Berlin
Haverkamp SST, Münster

MSR-Anlagen, GLT-DDC und Fassadensteuerung/Building management systems
Ingenieurbüro H. Köhler GmbH & Co. KG, Wiesbach
Landis & Staefer, Berlin

Konferenzraumtechnik/Conference room technology
Provideo Broadcast- u. Konferenztechnik mbH, Berlin

Aussenanlagen/Landscaping
Fa. Pohl Garten-, Landschafts- u. Sportplatzbau GmbH, Berlin

Zentrales Schliesssystem/Locks
Dt. Türschliessergesellschaft
Oscar Müller & Söhne GmbH & Co., Berlin

Verkehrsbeschilderung und Orientierungssysteme/Signage
G. K. Behrendt, Berlin

Besonderer Ausbau/Special construction
Interzone Kunst und Design GmbH & Co. KG, Berlin
Presentation Factory, Berlin
Chamäleon Service GmbH, Berlin
Mastbau Gartner GmbH, Berlin
Tischlerei Geppert, Ketzür

Projektbeteiligte
Projects credits

Bauherr/Client
GSW Gemeinnützige Siedlungs- und Wohnungsbau-Gesellschaft Berlin mbH,
Die Geschäftsführung: **Hans Jörg Duvigneau, Gero Luckow (bis 1995), Volker Esche, Dr. Heinz Wirries**
Der Bauausschuss: **Manfred Dommasch (Projektleiter), Uwe Hameyer, Dietmar Bock, Adolf Schürkotter, Heinz Behr, Karl-Erich Beerbaum, Wolfgang Krebs, GSW-Betriebsrat**
Projektbüro: **Marion Winter, Fred Konieczny**
Öffentlichkeitsarbeit: **Beatrice Kindler**

Bezirksamt Kreuzberg/District surveyor
Abt. Bauwesen, Hr. Schuster

Berliner Feuerwehr/Berlin fire brigade
Abt. Vorbeugender Brandschutz, Hr. Schneider

Architekten/Architects
sauerbruch hutton architekten, berlin/london, www.sauerbruchhutton.de

Wettbewerb/Competition
louisa hutton, matthias sauerbruch, juan lucas young, simon hart, nicola murphy, liz adams

Entwurf und Ausführungsplanung/Design development and detail design
louisa hutton, matthias sauerbruch

juan lucas young (project architect), jens ludloff, brian lilley, philip engelbrecht, anna bader-hardt, govert gerritsen, moritz theden

giovanna albretti, michail blösser, anne-françoise chollet, denise dih, christian galvão, iman ghazali, christopher hagmann, felix held, susanne hofmann, karl-friedrich hörnlein, heinz jirout, fredrik källström, jeff kirby, harvey langston-jones, claus marquart, matthias matschewski, roger mullin, florian öttl, wolfgang thiessen, andreas weber, stefan wirth

Modell/Model
Monath + Menzel, Berlin, Hamlyn Terry

Projektsteuerung/Project management
Harms & Partner, Berlin/Hannover, Carsten Timm, Klaus Rothermund

Ausschreibung und Projektüberwachung/Quantities and site supervision
Harms & Partner, Berlin/Hannover, Klaus Weigel, Robert Harms, Karin Pfau, Heike Abraham, Sven Ahlfeldt, Sören Mäge, Heinz Papendieck, Jörg Rauh, Andrzei Senger, Ilka Schuppert, Marina Siano, Gülüzar Yildiz

Haustechnik/Environmental engineering
Wettbewerb (Niedrigenergiekonzept)/Competition (low energy concept): **Ove Arup & Partners, London, Guy Battle**
Entwurf/Design development: **Arup GmbH, Berlin, Chris Trott**
Ausführung/Detail design: **ARGE IGH mbH, Berlin und Arup GmbH, Berlin, Brian Cody, G. Meiner, Kerstin Kühnel, Peter Schuft**
Altbau/Existing tower: **GSW, Peter Lentz, Klaus Eggert, Detlef Fruck, Frank-Rainer Behnecke**

Tragwerksplanung/Structural engineering
Wettbewerb/Competition: **Dewhurst MacFarlane and Partners/Ove Arup & Partners, London**
Entwurf/Design development: **Arup GmbH, Berlin, John Pilkington, Nils Clemmetsen, Ian Gardner**
Ausführung/Site supervision: ARGE Arup GmbH, Berlin with IGH mbH, Berlin, Lawrence Vye, Züblin TBK, Dr. Bachmann, Stuttgart

Fassadenberatung/Façade consultants
Emmer, Pfenninger + Partner, Münchenstein

Schallschutz und Akustik/Acoustic consultant
Akustik-Ingenieurbüro Moll, Berlin

Brandschutzberatung/Fire engineering
Hosser, Hass + Partner, Berlin

Landschaftsarchitekt/Landscape architect
ST raum a, Berlin
GSW Edmund Fischer-Schwabe

Bodengutachter/Geophysical engineer
Büro Müller-Kirchenbauer, Berlin

Sicherheitsberater/Security consultant
ATD - Überbetr. Sicherheits- und Umwelttechnischer Dienst, Berlin

Berater für Statik/Client consultant for structure
Mehlhorn Ingenieurgesellschaft mbH, Berlin

Prüfstatiker
Büro Dr. Franke, Berlin

Vermesser/Surveyor
Günther Noormann, Berlin

Prüfung Raumluftt./Building regs. consultant ventilation system
TPG Lehmann mbH, Berlin

Gutachter TGA/Client consultant services
Zibell, Willner & Partner, Köln

Beratung Winddach/Consultant membrane roof
Prof. Burkhardt, Braunschweig

Orientierungssysteme/Signage
Westerveld und Wagemann, Berlin/Amsterdam, Judith Miller

Matthias Sauerbruch

	Prof. Dipl. Ing. AA Dipl. ARB, Architekt BDA
	geboren 1955 in Konstanz, Deutschland
84	Diplome an der HdK, Berlin und Architectural Association, London
85–90	Unit Master an der Architectural Association, London
seit 89	eigenes Büro mit Louisa Hutton in London
seit 95	Professor an der Technischen Universität, Berlin
	Gastvorlesungen an zahlreichen Universitäten im In- und Ausland

Louisa Hutton

	BA (Hons), AA Dipl. RIBA, Architektin
	geboren 1957 in Norwich, England
80	First Class Honours Degree an der Bristol University
85	Diplom an der Architectural Association, London
87–90	Lehre am Croydon College of Art, Unit Master an der Architectural Association, London
seit 89	Büro mit Matthias Sauerbruch
	Gastvorlesungen an zahlreichen Universitäten im In- und Ausland

Juan Lucas Young

	UBA Dipl. Architekt
	geboren 1963 in Buenos Aires, Argentinien
89	Diplom an der Universidad de Buenos Aires
seit 90	Projektarchitekt bei sauerbruch hutton architekten
seit 99	Juniorpartner

Brian Lilley

	AA Dipl. RIBA, Architekt
	geboren 1958 in Calgary, Kanada
83	Bachelor of Enviromental Studies an der University of Manitoba, Kanada
88	Diplom an der Architectural Association, London
seit 93	Projektarchitek bei sauerbruch hutton architekten
seit 99	Juniorpartner

Jens Ludloff

	Dipl. Ing., Architekt
	geboren 1964 in Haan, Deutschland
87–94	Architekturstudium an der FH Münster
94	Diplom an der Polytechnischen Universität Krakau
seit 93	Projektarchitekt bei sauerbruch hutton architekten
seit 99	Juniorpartner

Matthias Sauerbruch

	Prof. Dipl. Ing., AA Dipl. ARB, Architect BDA
	born 1955 in Constance, Germany
84	Diplomas from the HdK Berlin and the Architectural Association, London
85–90	Unit Master at the Architectural Association, London
since 89	Office with Louisa Hutton
since 95	Professor at the Technical University, Berlin
	Guest Lecturer at many Universities nationally and internationally

Louisa Hutton

	BA (Hons), AA Dipl. RIBA
	born 1957 in Norwich, England
80	First Class Honours Degree from Bristol University
85	Diploma at the Architectural Association, London
87–90	Taught at Croydon College of Art, Unit Master at the Architectural Association, London
since 89	Office with Matthias Sauerbruch
	Guest Lecturer at many Universities nationally and internationally

Juan Lucas Young

	UBA Dipl. Architect
	born 63 in Buenos Aires, Argentina
89	Diploma at the Universidad de Buenos Aires
since 90	Project architect at sauerbruch hutton architects
since 99	Junior partner

Brian Lilley

	AA Dipl. RIBA, Architect
	born 1958 in Calgary, Canada
83	Bachelor of Enviromental Studies, University of Manitoba, Canada
88	Diploma at the Architectural Association, London
since 93	Project architect at sauerbruch hutton architects
since 99	Junior partner

Jens Ludloff

	Dipl. Ing., Architect
	born 1964 in Haan, Germany
87–94	Architecture Studies at FH Münster
94	Diploma at the Polytechnical University Krakau
since 93	Project architect at sauerbruch hutton architects
since 99	Junior partner

Projekte (Auswahl)

89–90 L-House, Umbau eines viktorianischen Hauses, London
Umbau eines georgianischen Hauses, London
91–99 GSW Hauptverwaltung, Berlin
94–95 Umbau eines viktorianischen Hauses, London
H-House, Umbau eines 60er-Jahre-Hauses, London
95–98 Photonikzentrum, Berlin
97–99 N-House, Umbau eines denkmalgeschützten Hauses, London
98–99 Zumtobel Staff Beratungszentrum, Berlin
99–00 British Council, Deutsche Hauptverwaltung, Information Centre und Sprachschule, Berlin
98–00 EFM, Experimentelle Fabrik Magdeburg, Sachsen-Anhalt (im Bau)
99– Umweltbundesamt Dessau (Planung)
Buch V, Niedrigenergiehaus zur Bauausstellung Berlin 1999 (Planung)
Polizeiabschnitt 35 und Feuerwache für das Parlaments- und Regierungsviertel in Berlin (Planung)
Verwaltungsgebäude für die Universität Hamburg (Planung)

Selected built projects

89–90 L-House, Conversion of a Victorian House, London
Conversion of a Georgian House, London
91–99 GSW Headquarters Building, Berlin
94–95 Conversion of a Victorian House, London
H-House, Conversion of a 1960's Villa, London
95–98 Photonics Centre, Berlin Adlershof
97–99 N-House, Conversion of a Historic House, London
98–99 Lighting Showroom for Zumtobel Staff, Berlin
99–00 British Council, German Headquarters, Information and Teaching Center, Berlin
98–00 EFM, Experimental Factory Magdeburg, Germany (under construction)
99– Federal Office for the Ministry of the Environment, Dessau (design stage)
New Loft Housing, Berlin (design stage)
Police and Fire Station for the Government District, Berlin (design stage)
University Administration Buildings, Hamburg (design stage)

Auszeichnungen (Auswahl)

96 AIA (London), Excellence in Design Award
98 Constructec-Preis für Europäische Industriearchitektur
Erich Schelling Architekturpreis
Architekturpreis der WestHyp-Stiftung für vorbildliche Gewerbebauten
99 Architektur Preis Beton 1999, Architekturpreis der deutschen Zementindustrie
Deutscher Architekturpreis 1999, Auszeichnung
RIBA Award, London
ar+d Award, High Commendation, London/Kopenhagen

Selected awards

96 AIA (London) Excellence in Design Award
98 Constructec Prize 1998 – European Prize for Industrial Architecture
Erich Schelling Architecture Prize
WestHyp Foundation Architecture Prize
99 Architektur Preis Beton 1999, Architecture Prize of the german cement industry
Deutscher Architekturpreis 1999, Berlin
RIBA Award, London
ar+d Award, High Commendation, London/Copenhagen

Monographien

92 Projekte 1989–1991 Katalog der Galerie Aedes, Berlin
96 Berlin Architecture in the New Landscape, Projects 1990–1996, Birkhäuser Verlag, Basel
98 Photonikzentrum Berlin Adlershof (Ausstellungskatalog), Weissenhof Galerie, Stuttgart
99 WYSIWYG (Ausstellungskatalog), Architectural Association, London
00 Das UBA in Dessau (Ausstellungskatalog), Berlin

Monographs

92 Aedes catalogue, Berlin
96 Architecture in the New Landscape, Projects 1990–1996, Birkhäuser Verlag, Basel
98 Photonics Centre, Berlin (exhibition catalogue), Weissenhof Gallery, Stuttgart
99 WYSIWYG (exhibition catalogue), Architectural Association, London
00 Das UBA in Dessau (exhibiton catologue), Berlin

Bildnachweis
Illustration credits

Bitter + Bredt 8, 9, 10, 15, 16, 18, 19, 20, 21, 66, 68, 70, 71, 72, 84, 86, 90 (1, 2), 94, 96, 104, 108, 109, 110 (2), 116, 120, 126, 130, 152, 154, 160, 162, 163, 196 (1), 214, 222, 225, 228, 232, 244, 247

Annette Kisling 2, 14, 26, 64, 79, 100, 111 (2), 112, 118, 119, 121, 132, 139, 142, 148, 158, 166 (1,2), 167 (1, 2), 172, 174 (1, 2), 175, 176, 179 (3), 181 (1), 184, 185, 186, 188, 196 (2), 198, 199 (2), 215, 216, 218, 219 (1, 2), 224, 231, 248

Erik Jan Ouwerkerk 76, 77 (1, 2), 81, 88, 89, 122 (1, 2), 123, 135 (1), 151, 200, 221, 226

Ove Arup & Partners 57, 189 (1), 190, 191, 192, 193

Lepkowski & Hillmann 110 (1), 111 (1), 164

Reinhard Görner 58, 60, 146, 208

ME & Company 168, 169

Barthelme/Götz GmbH 210

Robert Frank 35 (3)

Barbara Noculak 73

Krause/Eternit AG 149

Borutta-Foto 32 (3)

Ullstein Bilddienst/Heinz O. Durisch 29 (8)

University of Bristol, Department of Aerospace Engineering 207 (1, 2)

Foto: Landesbildstelle Berlin 24, 28 (1, 2, 4), 29 (5, 6, 7, 10), 31 (1), 32 (1, 2), 34, 149 (2)

Mit Erlaubnis der Senatsverwaltung für Stadtentwicklung-III-: Ausschnitt aus *Plan von der Königl: Residentz Stadt Berlin*, 1723, gezeichnet von G. Dusableau 30, Ausschnitt aus *Plan de la Ville de Berlin*, 1748 von Graf von Schmettau 31 (2), Ausschnitt aus dem *Liebenow-Plan*, 1888 31 (3), Bildflug 1953, russische Luftaufnahmen 33

Gefatec Gesellschaft für Fassadentechnik mbH 105 (1)

Götz GmbH 220, 230

Ed. Züblin AG 178, 180 (1)

Wöhr + Bauer GmbH 80

Stahl- + Verbundbau 138 (1)

Architekturwerkstatt, Helge Pitz 237

Architekturbüro Brenner & Tonnon 241

sauerbruch hutton architekten, wenn nicht anders erwähnt

Impressum

Konzept und Redaktion/concept and editorial staff
sauerbruch hutton architekten, Matthias Sauerbruch,
Louisa Hutton, Isabelle Hartmann

Übersetzungen/translation
sauerbruch hutton architekten

Gestaltung/cover design, layout and typeface
Integral Lars Müller, Lars Müller, Christian Schuler,
Esther Schütz

Litho/picture scanning and retouching
artificial image, Michael Maria Müller, Vivian Weiss,
Ute Reinelt, Heike Buchfelder

Druck/printing
Medialis Offsetdruck GmbH, Werner Franz

ISBN 3-907078-14-4

Lars Müller Publishers
5401 Baden, Switzerland
books@lars-muller.ch

Wir danken folgenden Firmen für die finanzielle Unterstützung/we thank the following firms for their financial support:

GSW Gemeinnützige Siedlungs- und Wohnungsbau-Gesellschaft Berlin mbH

Gefatec Gesellschaft für Fassadentechnik mbH, Berlin

Wini Büromöbel, Coppenbrügge

Harms & Partner, Hannover

Bolwin & Heemann, Steinhagen

Elektrobau Peter Schulze GmbH, Berlin

Eternit Aktiengesellschaft, Berlin

Götz GmbH, Ludwigsburg

Arup GmbH, Berlin

Bilfinger und Berger, Berlin

Arge Rohbau GSW Hauptverwaltung Ed. Züblin AG, Berlin

Ed. Züblin AG, Stuttgart

Wilkhahn Wilkening + Hahne GmbH & Co.

Wöhr + Bauer GmbH, München

Akustik-Ingenieurbüro Moll, Berlin